GOD, THE BRAIN, THE BIBLE A

GOD, THE BRAIN, THE BIBLE AND YOUR BODY

Published by

www.lulu.com

Copyright © 2017 by Zoser Research Society
ISBN 978-1-365-75028-1

Front and back cover by Tehuti Re
Painted pictures by Emhotep Gerald Richards at
www.nuwbia.com

All rights reserved. No part of this book may be reproduced, stored in retrieval system, or transmitted in any form, by any means, including mechanical, electronic, photocopying, recording, or otherwise without prior written permission of the publisher.

Printed in the United States of America

GOD, THE BRAIN, THE BIBLE AND YOUR BODY

Books Authored

African Origin Found in Religion and Freemasonry Part I

African Origin Found in Religion and Freemasonry Part II

Religion, Politics, and Freemasonry: A violent attack against ancient Africa

Do Freemasons worship Lucifer?

The Debate: Zoser Research Society vs. Phylaxis Research Society Prince Hall Affiliation

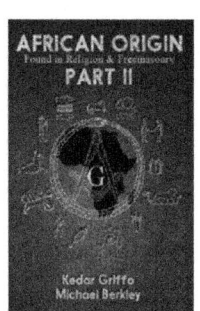

ABOUT THE AUTHOR

Kedar Griffo is a master communicator and multidimensional teacher/mentor. He has a worldwide speaking platform that has astonished crowds. He is the founder of Zoser Research Society and has authored more than five books specializing in religion, freemasonry, politics, foreign affairs and the economy. Dr. Griffo received his honorary Doctor of Divinity in Comparative Religious Studies from Holy Tabernacle Ministries and is also a decorated desert storm veteran with over 28 years of public service.

Dedication

This book is dedicated to my Goddess, who has encouraged, supported, loved me and gave me the space to complete this offering. You are appreciated more than you know.

Author's Acknowledgments

There are so many people to praise and thank. I want to thank Nia Damali, owner of Medu bookstore, for always providing a platform to lecture and sale books. I want to recognized DeWayne Hendrix, Dirk Johnson, Trineka (Trey) Hardy and Nu Ankh Radio for giving me a platform to pass along information to our people. I want to acknowledge Dr. Brenda L. Bronner and her shows "Brenation Presents" and "Bring Love Back" for allowing me to present this information on the small screen. My gratitude to Shelley Wynter for allowing me to express my political and economic views on his website www.shelleywinter.com. I am forever indebted to the ancestors for leaving this information for us to rediscover via their appointed teacher, the sacred master Paa Nabab Yaanuwn. We thank them for reintroducing us to the greater as well as lesser mysteries. Lastly, I want to thank you, the reader, for purchasing this scroll.

GOD, THE BRAIN, THE BIBLE AND YOUR BODY

Contents at a Glance Introduction

Chapter 1 – The Zodiac   Page 9

Chapter 2 – The Brain and the Bible   Page 21

Chapter 3 – Religious Books are Sexual in Nature Page 67

Chapter 4 – Chakras Page 81

Chapter 5 – Misinterpreted Symbols Page 93

Chapter 6 - Snake Handlers Page 99

Chapter 7 – Yearly Life Cycles Page 123

GOD, THE BRAIN, THE BIBLE AND YOUR BODY

FOREWARD

The author's aim is to bring awareness to the various subliminal as well as overt messages used by occultists as well as those who study the metaphysical. These messages are all around us yet are disquised as things that are both familiar and unfamiliar to our conscious mind. After reading and studying the pages of this book, the reader will begin to notice the symbolism that has surrounded their environment their entire lifetime yet were unaware of the hidden messages. The reader will also recognize how important the Sun, moon and stars have been to the success of corporations, persons and entities.

The Zodiac

The Holy Bible is one of the most read books in the entire world. Various groups use it for numerous purposes, thus each group views it differently than the others, which has led to diverse interpretations of its meaning. A monk named John Cassian (360-435) identified four ways in which the bible could be understood: literal, symbolic, ethical and mystical. The literal approach takes the bible at face value. This view is the most flawed because of verses like Psalms 98:8, which imply the rivers/floods, clap their hands. A better and more practical approach to reading the bible is the symbolic method. The bible also gives an example as found in the book of Galatians 4:22-31 where the Apostle Paul wrote the story about Abraham and his two wives, Hagar and Sarah, here again this could be read allegorically. The third way of interpreting the Bible is to look for an 'ethical' meaning. This method utilizes the moral senses of applying biblical verses to one's everyday life. Certain Jewish groups refer to this method as Midrash. Again, the bible gives an example in 1st Corinthians 9 where Paul compares a quote in the Old Testament regarding oxen and later explains the real context of this verse. Mythical is the fourth way to interpret the bible. This methodology involves interpreting text to reveal future events as found in the book of Revelations. Another kind of mystical interpretation involves finding secret codes called Kabbalistic. This is a very mystical interpretation, which finds meanings with numbers and symbols. The biblical patriarch Abraham and his sons Isaac and Jacob are said to stand for the emotions of love, fear and mercy respectively. Author: Bible Society, 20 March 2016 (Last updated: 21 July 2016)

Sarah and Hagar

The author of this work also suggests there are three additional ways to view and read the bible eschatological, physiological, and astrological. Eschatological deals with the end of the world end of time concept. The physiological way is known as the newest way to interpret the bible; however, the author feels it was the original way the bible should be interpreted. According to dictionary.com, physiology is defined as the branch of biology dealing with the functions and activities of living organisms and their parts, including all physical and chemical processes. Thus the author believes the bible was written to teach you to know yourself not only spiritually but physically as well to ensure you have a long life. Whereas the book of John states in John 10:10 in part... I am come that they might have life, and that they might have it more abundantly. This view will be discussed in detail in later chapters of this book. The last and final way to interpret the bible is an old and forgotten method that is making resurgence is the method of astrology. This method is currently being referred to as astro-theology and deals with the "as above so below" axiom or as the Lord's Prayer says "thy will be done in heaven as it is in earth".

Unfortunately, the religious world has ostracized Astrology, calling it a pseudo-science and saying it is not of God. However, the bible seems to see things other than organized religion. The bible condemns astrologers not astrology, the same way it condemned lawyers not the law. "And he said, Woe unto you also, ye lawyers! for ye lade men with burdens grievous to be borne, and ye yourselves touch not the burdens with one of your fingers" (King James Version, Luke 11.46)." The word zodiac is mentioned in the bible as the word Mazzaroth. According to the Strong's concordance, Mazzaroth is defined as the 12 signs of the Zodiac and their 36 associated constellations.

mazzârâh, maz-zaw-raw'; apparently from H5144 in the sense of distinction; some noted constellation (only in the plural), perhaps collectively, the zodiac:—

Mazzoroth. Compare H4208.
http://www.eliyah.com/lexicon.html,Web

Astrology is the study of the celestial bodies, their movements and how those movements influence human affairs; therefore, based on this definition the bible agrees. The book of Psalms says that God named the stars " telleth the number of the stars; he calleth them all by their names"(Psalms 147.4). Other places such as Genesis says let the stars be for signs, and accordingly states "And God said, Let there be lights in the firmament of the heaven to divide the day from the night; and let them be for signs, and for seasons, and for days, and years."(Gen 1.14) Strong's concordance defines signs from the Hebrew word 'ôwth, oth; probably from H225 (in the sense of appearing); a signal (literally or figuratively), as a flag, beacon, monument, omen, prodigy, evidence, etc.:—mark, miracle, (en-) sign, token. So now, we have God naming the stars and then saying let them be for signs. Jesus said that in the time of the end there will be a sign in the sky, "the sign of the Son of man in heaven" (Matthew 24.30), The other part of the definition is that these celestial objects influence you. The book of Job says that there are star constellations that influence you. It is stated Canst thou bind the sweet influences of Pleiades, or loose the bands of Orion? 32 Canst thou bring forth Mazzaroth in his season? or canst thou guide Arcturus with his sons? Pleiades, Orion and Arcturus are star constellations; (Job 38.31-32) Pleiades and Orion both are seven star constellations coincidently. In other books it says to "Seek him that maketh the seven stars and Orion, and turneth the shadow of death into the morning, and maketh the day dark with night: that calleth for the waters of the sea, and poureth them out upon the face of the earth: The LORD is his name:"(Amos 5.8) Additionally, we find the following; By his spirit he hath garnished the heavens; his hand hath formed the crooked serpent. (Job 26.13) The crooked serpent is the Milky Way, which looks like a snake with its tail in its mouth. This has been illustrated as the Oroborous in Egypt.

Oroborous

Therefore, to recap we have astrology defined as the science of the celestial bodies and how they influence us, and the bible is saying there are stars that influence us as well as actually using the word mazzaroth a term meaning zodiac. The zodiac is comprised of 12 different star systems and each zodiac sign has separate characteristics from the other 11. Coincidently, the male tribes of both Ishmael and Israel both number twelve. Each tribe represents a different characteristic just as the zodiac signs. **1** And Jacob called unto his sons, and said, Gather yourselves together, that I may tell you that which shall befall you in the last days. **2** Gather yourselves together, and hear, ye sons of Jacob; and hearken unto Israel your father. **3** Reuben, thou art my firstborn, my might, and the beginning of my strength, the excellency of dignity, and the excellency of power: **4** Unstable as water, thou shalt not excel; because thou wentest up to thy father's bed; then defiledst thou it: he went up to my couch. **5** Simeon and Levi are brethren; instruments of cruelty are in their habitations. **6** O my soul, come not thou into their secret; unto their assembly, mine honour, be not thou united: for in their anger they slew a man, and in their selfwill they digged down a wall. **7** Cursed be their anger, for it was fierce; and their wrath, for it was cruel: I will divide them in Jacob, and scatter them in Israel. **8** Judah, thou art he whom thy brethren shall praise: thy hand shall be in the neck of thine enemies; thy father's children shall bow down before thee. **9** Judah is a lion's whelp: from the prey, my son, thou art gone up: he stooped down, he couched as a lion, and as an old lion; who shall rouse him up? **10** The sceptre shall not depart from Judah, nor a lawgiver from between his feet, until Shiloh come; and unto him shall the gathering of the people be. **11** Binding his foal unto the vine, and his ass's colt unto the choice vine; he washed his garments in wine, and his clothes in the blood of grapes: **12** His eyes shall be red with wine, and his teeth white with milk. **13** Zebulun shall dwell at the haven of the sea; and he shall be for an haven of ships; and his border shall be unto Zidon. **14** Issachar is a strong ass couching down between two burdens: **15** And he saw that rest was good, and the land that it was pleasant; and bowed his shoulder to bear, and became a servant unto tribute. **16** Dan shall judge his people, as one of the tribes of Israel. **17** Dan shall be a serpent by the way, an adder in the path, that biteth the horse heels, so that his rider shall fall backward. **18** I have waited for thy salvation, O LORD. **19** Gad, a troop shall overcome him: but he shall overcome at the last. **20** Out of Asher his bread shall be fat, and he shall yield royal dainties. **21** Naphtali is a hind let loose: he giveth goodly words. **22** Joseph is a fruitful bough, even a fruitful bough by a well; whose branches run over the wall: **23** The archers have sorely grieved him, and shot at him, and hated him: **24** But his bow abode in strength, and the arms of his hands were made strong by the hands of the mighty God of Jacob; (from thence is the shepherd, the stone of Israel:) **25** Even by the God of thy father, who shall help thee; and by the Almighty, who shall bless thee with blessings of heaven above, blessings of the deep that lieth under, blessings of the breasts, and of the womb: **26** The blessings of thy father have prevailed above the blessings of my progenitors unto the utmost bound of the everlasting hills: they shall be on the head of Joseph, and on the crown of the head of him that was separate from his brethren. **27** Benjamin shall ravin as a wolf: in the morning he shall devour the prey, and at night he shall divide the spoil. **28** All these are the twelve tribes of Israel: and this is it that their father spake unto them, and blessed them; every one according to his blessing he blessed them. (Gen 49.1-28)

Tribe of Israel	Zodiac
Reuben	Aquarius
Simon	Gemini
Levi	Gemini
Judah	Leo
Issachar	Taurus
Zebulun	Pisces
Dan	Scorpio
Naphtali	Capricorn
Gad	Aries
Asher	Libra
Joseph	Sagittarius
Benjamin	Cancer
Dinah	Virgo

As the reader studies the characteristics of the twelve tribes, they will notice the similarities with the twelve signs of the zodiac. In Rupert Gleadow's book The Origin of The Zodiac, the author quotes a 9th century monk by the name of Helpericus, who speculated on the origin of the names of the Zodiac signs: *"Aquarius and Pisces are explained by the rainy season, Leo by the heat, and Libra by the equinox; in Cancer the Sun begins to move backwards (like a crab). The Scorpion's sting and the Archer's arrow are both compared to the sting of hailshowers, and Capricorn is the lower turning point of the sun because goats graze uphill. The Ram, however, was either named because the sun breaks up the frozen earth as a ram attacks with its horns, or else because rams, having slept on the their left side all the winter, now start to sleep on their right. In the month of Taurus oxen work to prepare the ripening of the corn, but the explanation of Gemini is an incoherent allusion to Castor and Pollux. Virgo finally is so called because the earth is exhausted and no longer bears any fruit – the transition from the pretty girl to the old maid on the way."*

We can see how these names intimately fit the seasonal changes in weather and agriculture. Additionally, these zodiac signs can affect our health and individuals not familiar with the zodiac tend to dismiss generic zodiac readings. The author understands this perspective yet offers an explanation of how each zodiac sign is comprised of 30 degree and is a 1/12th of a 360 degree circle and these degrees are subdivided into 12 decans each. Twelve multiplied by thirty is three hundred sixty degrees representing a circle; therefore, if you take the first zodiac sign Aries and divide into three sections you will end up with three different personalities for that sign. This accounts for why no two people with the same zodiac sign have the exact same personality. Aries begins on the spring equinox of March 21, ten days from March 21 will give you the first decan. April 1 to April 10 will give you the second decan and the last decan is April 10-19. Therefore, each person born under the sign of Aries will vary in personality traits. Additionally, the same concept applies to how the zodiac affects people. Some people are inclined to specific medical issues based on when they were born, yet again this is not inclusive for all. Famed Greek physician Hippocrates stated a physician without a knowledge of

GOD, THE BRAIN, THE BIBLE AND YOUR BODY

Astrology has no right to call himself a physician. Therefore, it should be used in the application of curing and healing the human body. For example, the moon is known to affect waters on the planet earth. Additionally, it also affects the water inside of human beings. This in turn has been incorporated into learning when and how one should have corrective medical procedures as having the moon in the wrong sign during surgery could cause one to hemorrhage because of the moon's effect on blood in the body. When the moon is in the sign of Leo, one should not have heart surgery as Leo rules the heart. Another example would be when the moon is in Capricorn you should not have surgery on your knees or skeletal system. Below are some maladies that affect the various zodiac signs:

Aries – stress in hypothalamus, pituitary and pineal gland , tightness in the head, severe headaches, pressure within the eyes, dryness of scalp and skin, eruptions on the face, and ringing in the ears

Taurus – kidney stones, kidney problems, headaches, urinary tract infections, gall bladder problems, tonsillitis, and varicose veins

Gemini – insomnia, speech problems, random thoughts, central nervous system problems, inability to relax–digestive problems, acidic condition, and breakdown of teeth enamel

GOD, THE BRAIN, THE BIBLE AND YOUR BODY

Leo – stress in heart region, fluctuating blood pressure, sense of fatigue, heart muscle tissue break down, and fluctuating iron levels

Virgo – deep stress and fear of ones well-being, hypochondriac, thought confusion and hyper activity, and strange psychological systems

Libra – ear problems, excessive wax, ringing in the ear, dizziness, balance, low and mid back problems

Scorpio – trouble in pancreas, liver and colon, viruses and bacterial problems, intestinal, and infections in the glands

Sagittarius – thyroid problems, pituitary glands, and sciatic problems affecting the legs and feet

Capricorn – stress in the skeletal system, back problems, arthritis, spinal curvature, tooth decay, pituitary and thyroid problems, skin eruptions and cysts

Aquarius – problems with central nervous system, nerve diseases, skin disorders, brain disorders, severe headaches, and numbness in certain portions of the body

Pisces – immune system problems, extreme sensitivity to food and things that touch the skin, abnormal sensitivity to sunlight, discoloration of the skin because of sun light, skin cancers and reactions to chemicals in food and early puberty

GOD, THE BRAIN, THE BIBLE AND YOUR BODY

If you know someone who is affected by any of these medical conditions, it is possible it could be because of when they were born.

Virgo

The stars were eventually anthropomorphized into human beings. Notice how the constellation Virgo is shaped like the mother breastfeeding her infant son. This concept started in Africa and circled the world.

Sumerian	*Translation*	Modern name
GU.AN.NA	Heavenly Bull	Taurus
MASH.TAB.BA	Twins	Gemini
DUB	Pincers, Tongs	Cancer
UR.GULA	Lion	Leo
AB.SIN	Her father was Sin	Virgo
ZI.BA.AN.NA	Heavenly Fate	Libra
GIR.TAB	Which claws and cuts	Scorpio
PA.BIL (Archer)	Defender	Sagittarius
SUHUR.MASH	Goat-Fish	Capricorn
GU	Lord of the waters	Aquarius
SIM.MAH	Fishes	Pisces
KU.MAL	Field dweller	Aries

20

GOD, THE BRAIN, THE BIBLE AND YOUR BODY

The Brain and the Bible

"All the gods are three: Amun, Ra and Ptah, who have no equals. He whose nature [literally – whose name] is mysterious, being Amun; Ra is the head, Ptah the body. Their cities on earth, established forever are: Thebes, Heliopolis and Memphis [stable] for eternity. When a message comes from heaven, it is heard at Heliopolis, it is repeated at Memphis to Ptah and it is made into a letter written in the letters of Thoth [at Hermopolis] for the city of Amun [Thebes] ." The Leyden Papyrus. "*Of God and Gods*", Jan Assmann. p. 64, University of Wisconsin Press, 2008, ISBN 978-0-299-22554-4

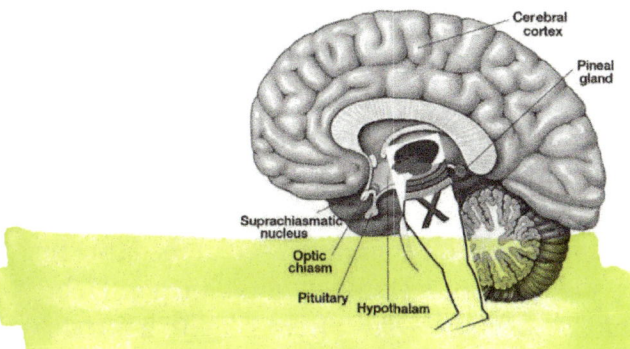

Ptah in the brain

The aim of this chapter is show the relationship of the human body to the various religious texts using the physiological approach. As noted above the Leyden papyrus shows how the three Gods; Amun, Ra and Ptah are synonymous with various parts of the body. Inside of our brains is the putamen, an organ that regulates

GOD, THE BRAIN, THE BIBLE AND YOUR BODY

movement and facilitates learning. As you see this is a play on the two Tama-Re or Egyptian gods Ptah and Amun (Amen). The putamen is connected to the caudate nucleus and globus palladus and these three assist with movement and learning just as the Gods, Amun, Ra and Ptah are one. All religions wrote in coded language to keep those not initiated into the mysteries or the uninitiated out but those who subdued their passions by going within were given the keys to the kingdom of God. As you take this long journey via a short path, we start by examining the bible. The bible is written in codes, one of those codes is the anatomy of the body and the functions of the brain. However before we go there, lets show you the various quotes in the bible that show it is a book of allegory, parables, dark sayings. The word parable comes from the Hebrew word mashal. According to Strong's concordance, mâshâl, maw-shawl'; apparently from H4910 in some original sense of superiority in mental action; properly, a pithy maxim, usually of metaphorical nature; hence, a simile (as an adage, poem, discourse):—byword, like, parable, proverb. Another word commonly used in the bible but omitted by theologians is Dark Sayings which in Hebrew is the word Chiydah khee-daw'; from H2330; a puzzle, hence, a trick, conundrum, sententious maxim:—dark saying (sentence, speech), hard question, proverb, riddle. According to this definition a dark saying is a riddle. You find the use of the word dark sayings where it states; I will open my mouth in a parable: I will utter dark sayings of old: 3 Which we have heard and known, and our fathers have told us. (Psalms 78.2) As well as "To understand a proverb, and the interpretation; the

22

words of the wise, and their dark sayings. It should be clear to the reader parables and dark sayings are one in the same." (Proverbs 1.6) Other biblical verses that speak about parables are found in the books of Psalms and Ezekiel. " I will incline mine ear to a parable: I will open my dark saying upon the harp. (Psalms 49.4); Son of man, put forth a riddle, and speak a parable unto the house of Israel; (Ezekiel 17.2) Then said I, Ah Lord GOD! they say of me, Doth he not speak parables? (Ezekiel 20.49) Now that we have an understanding of what a parable or dark saying means we must now reexamine the things we have read in the bible and start to look for riddles, hidden meanings, and secret knowledge. New Testament writer Paul says in his letter to the Corinthians: But we speak the wisdom of God in a mystery, even the hidden wisdom, which God ordained before the world unto our glory. (1 Cor 2.7) This teaches us there is a mystery to the word of God and since this is true, we must find keys to understanding what the bible is really trying to convey. When the disciples of Jesus came to him and asked him why he spoke to the crowd in parables, Jesus explained his reason for doing so in Matthew Who hath ears to hear, let him hear. 10 And the disciples came, and said unto him, Why speakest thou unto them in parables? 11 He answered and said unto them, Because it is given unto you to know the mysteries of the kingdom of heaven, but to them it is not given. 12 For whosoever hath, to him shall be given, and he shall have more abundance: but whosoever hath not, from him shall be taken away even that he hath. 13 Therefore speak I to them in parables: because they seeing see not; and hearing they hear not, neither do they understand. 14 And in them is fulfilled the prophecy of Esaias, which saith, By hearing ye shall hear, and shall not understand; and seeing ye shall see, and shall not perceive: 15 For this people's heart is waxed gross, and their ears are dull of hearing, and their eyes they have closed; lest at any time they should see with their eyes, and hear with their ears, and should understand with their heart, and should be converted, and I should heal them. 16 But blessed are your eyes, for they see: and your ears, for they hear. (Matt.13:9-15)

So here, Jesus is telling the disciples he gave them the mystery to the kingdom of heaven but he did not give it to the people as he felt they would not understand because their hearts have been waxed. We also find in Mark where it states And with many such parables spake he the word unto them, as they were able to hear it. But without a parable spake he not unto them: and when they were alone, he expounded all things to his disciples. (Matt.4.33-34) Here we find that when the people would leave and it was just Jesus and his disciples he would explain the dark saying so they would understand the keys to the kingdom of God. He told the disciples he would give them the key maphtêach, maf-tay'-akh; from H6605; an opener, i.e. a key:—key. And I will give unto thee the keys of the kingdom of heaven: and whatsoever thou shalt bind on earth shall be bound in heaven: and whatsoever thou shalt loose on earth shall be loosed in heaven. I will give unto you the keys to the kingdom of heaven. (Matt. 16.19) What is this key you ask? The key is simply the kingdom of God is within you. No, it is not in outer space it is right inside of your

GOD, THE BRAIN, THE BIBLE AND YOUR BODY

body! This is initially mentioned in the book of Isaiah, which states and the key of the house of David will I lay upon his shoulder; so he shall open, and none shall shut; and he shall shut, and none shall open. (Isa. 22.22) He admonishes the Judaic lawmakers of his time telling them they prevented the people from going inside to look for the Kingdom of Heaven. Woe unto you, lawyers! for ye have taken away the key of knowledge: ye entered not in yourselves, and them that were entering in ye hindered. (Luke 11.52),

We have been taught that we should go to church, a temple, and mosque to find God. However, the bible teaches that God dwells in the body and not in temples made with hands according to Acts. Howbeit the most High dwelleth not in temples made with hands; as saith the prophet, (Acts 7.48) additionally, we find in 1st Corinthians don't you know you are the temple of god and the spirit of god dwells in you. (1 Cor. 3.16) Jesus said And when he was demanded of the Pharisees, when the kingdom of God should come, he answered them and said, The kingdom of God cometh not with observation: 21 Neither shall they say, Lo here! or, lo there! for, behold, the kingdom of God is within you. (Luke 17.20)

The question now is how do you make contact with the spirit and kingdom of God that dwells within? Again, the bible gives us the answers as it says this book of the law shall not depart out of thy mouth; but thou shalt meditate therein day and night, that thou mayest observe to do according to all that is written therein: for then thou shalt make thy way prosperous, and then thou shalt have good success. (Josh. 1.8)   Meditation is the way to make contact with the spirit of God and the Kingdom of God. Meditation is prescribed and found throughout the bible.

First, let us define meditation. Meditation is defined as *1*: to engage in contemplation or reflection *2*: to engage in mental exercise (as concentration on one's breathing or repetition of a mantra) for the purpose of reaching a heightened level of spiritual awareness by the Merriam-Webster dictionary. https://www.merriam-webster.com/dictionary/meditate. Meditation comes from the Latin word meditatio which comes from a verb meditari meaning to think, contemplate, devise and ponder. *An universal etymological English dictionary* 1773, London, by Nathan Bailey ISBN 1-00-237787-0. Note: from the 1773 edition on Google books, not earlier editions. The author does not intend to instruct the reader on every type and form of meditation as they are too numerous to name. Other forms of meditation do not involve sitting still in contemplation these are the moving meditation techniques called tai chi and qigong. The author will only give the benefits of meditation. Meditation can transform our mind from negative to positive, from disturbed to peaceful, from unhappy to happy. Other measured benefits of meditation include lowering blood pressure, improving blood circulation, lowering your heart rate. In addition it also slows the respiratory rate, lower's the blood cortisol levels while simultaneously leaves the practitioner feeling less stressed with deeper relaxation and more feelings of well-being. Meditation has been looked at as an eastern practice, yet we must also realize the origins of Christianity and other Abrahamic faiths are eastern in nature and origin. Thus, we should keep an open mind about this ancient practice as soon the reader will embark upon numerous scriptures in the bible that speak of meditation. In keeping with the theme of the book, we will deal with the type of meditation that is biblically based. Eastern Orthodox Christians practice a form of meditation called Hesychasm. Hesychasm supposedly originates based on Jesus telling the people to meditate But thou, when thou prayest, enter into thy closet, and when thou hast shut thy door, pray to thy Father which is in secret; and thy Father which seeth in secret shall reward thee openly. (Matt. 6.6) This is just one of the times meditation is mentioned in the bible, here are other examples.

Gen.24;63] And Isaac went out to meditate in the field at the eventide: and he lifted up his eyes, and saw, and, behold, the camels were coming.

Pss.1:[2] But his delight is in the law of the LORD; and in his law doth he meditate day and night.

Pss.63:[6] When I remember thee upon my bed, and meditate on thee in the night watches.

Pss.77:[12] I will meditate also of all thy work, and talk of thy doings.

Pss.119: [15] I will meditate in thy precepts, and have respect unto thy ways.

GOD, THE BRAIN, THE BIBLE AND YOUR BODY

[23] Princes also did sit and speak against me: but thy servant did meditate in thy statutes.

[48] My hands also will I lift up unto thy commandments, which I have loved; and I will meditate in thy statutes.

[78] Let the proud be ashamed; for they dealt perversely with me without a cause: but I will meditate in thy precepts.

[148] Mine eyes prevent the night watches, that I might meditate in thy word.

Pss.143 [5] I remember the days of old; I meditate on all thy works; I muse on the work of thy hands.

Isa.33 [18] Thine heart shall meditate terror. Where is the scribe? where is the receiver? where is he that counted the towers?

Luke.21 [14] Settle it therefore in your hearts, not to meditate before what ye shall answer:

1Tim.4 [15] Meditate upon these things; give thyself wholly to them; that thy profiting may appear to all.

Another way to say meditate in the bible is the use of the words daily sacrifice.

Dan.8:[11] Yea, he magnified himself even to the prince of the host, and by him the daily sacrifice was taken away, and the place of his sanctuary was cast down.

[12] And an host was given him against the daily sacrifice by reason of transgression, and it cast down the truth to the ground; and it practised, and prospered.

[13] Then I heard one saint speaking, and another saint said unto that certain saint which spake, How long shall be the vision concerning the daily sacrifice, and the transgression of desolation, to give both the sanctuary and the host to be trodden under foot?

Dan.11

[31] And arms shall stand on his part, and they shall pollute the sanctuary of strength, and shall take away the daily sacrifice, and they shall place the abomination that maketh desolate.

Dan.12

[11] And from the time that the daily sacrifice shall be taken away, and the abomination that maketh desolate set up, there shall be a thousand two hundred and ninety days.

GOD, THE BRAIN, THE BIBLE AND YOUR BODY

Meditation has been demonized in the churches as some far eastern mysticism that is the work of the devil. However, the bible not only promotes but also clearly condones meditation. Those preachers who speak negatively about meditation are the same ones Jesus spoke about Woe unto you, lawyers! for ye have taken away the key of knowledge: ye entered not in yourselves, and them that were entering in ye hindered. (Luke 11.52)

GOD, THE BRAIN, THE BIBLE AND YOUR BODY

The author's aim is to show you how the bible is actually telling you God dwells in the body and specifically the brain and much of what you read in the bible is code or symbolism for the human body, which relates to the stars above. Here are a few biblical verses that teach the reader not to take the bible literally but metaphysically or as previously stated by using parables and dark sayings. I will open my mouth in a parable: I will utter dark sayings of old: (Psalms 78.2) To understand a proverb, and the interpretation; the words of the wise, and their dark sayings. (Proverbs 1.6) But without a parable spake he not unto them: and when they were alone, he expounded all things to his disciples. (Mark 4.34) Which things are an allegory: for these are the two covenants; the one from the mount Sinai, which gendereth to bondage, which is Agar (Gal. 4.24) and Who also hath made us able ministers of the new testament; not of the letter, but of the spirit: for the letter killeth, but the spirit giveth life. (2 Cor. 2.6) As you see in these verses, the bible was not meant to be taken literally but was written to make the reader inquire deeper into the mysteries. And he said unto them, Unto you it is given to know the mystery of the kingdom of God: but unto them that are without, all these things are done in parables. (Mark 4.11) Alternatively, it states But we speak the wisdom of God in a mystery, even the hidden wisdom, which God ordained before the world unto our glory: (1 Cor. 2.7)

As we take this long journey on a short path, we begin to explore the mysteries and request the reader to remember what you read ain't always what you read. According to

GOD, THE BRAIN, THE BIBLE AND YOUR BODY

Genesis And a river went out of Eden to water the garden; and from thence it was parted, and became into four heads. (Gen. 2.10) Biblical scholars have identified the Tigris/Euphrates River as one of the rivers mentioned here, and the remaining are the Hiddekel, Gihon, and Pishon, which would make it four rivers. Yet as we turn to the anatomy of the human brain via Stedman's medical dictionary it says; between the arachnoid layer of the brain and the pia mater flows a river of cerebral spinal fluid that bathes the brain and provides a soft fluid protective cushion. The cerebral fluid originates from the walls of an interconnected cave located deep within the brain. The chambers of this cave, the ventricles, are four."

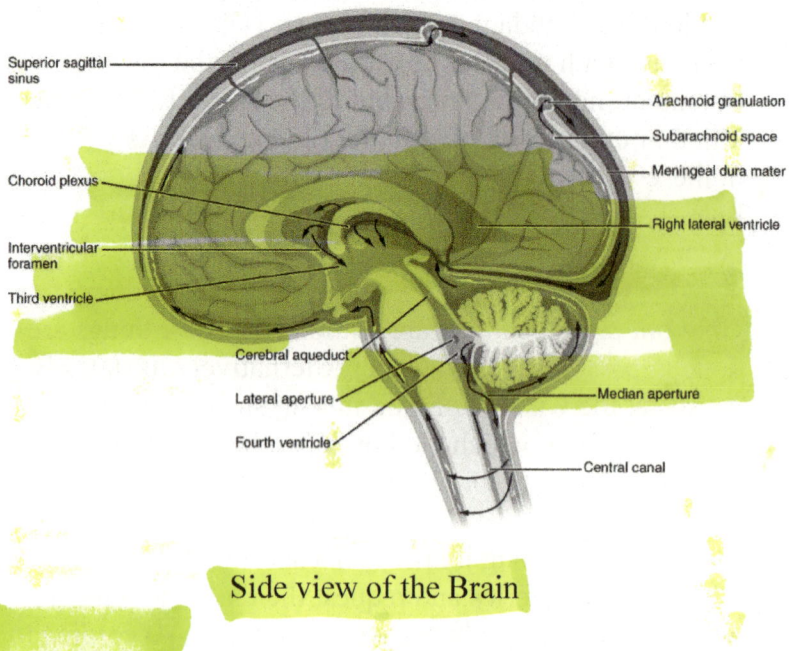

Side view of the Brain

These four cavities are the four ventricles found within the brain. The cavities of the hollow human brain are called ventricles. There are four ventricles in the human brain: two lateral ventricles in the cerebrum (largest ventricles of brain); the third ventricle in the diencephalon of the forebrain between the right and left thalamus; and the fourth ventricle located posterior to the pons and upper half of medulla of the hindbrain. The ventricles are concerned with the production and circulation of cerebrospinal fluid (CSF).

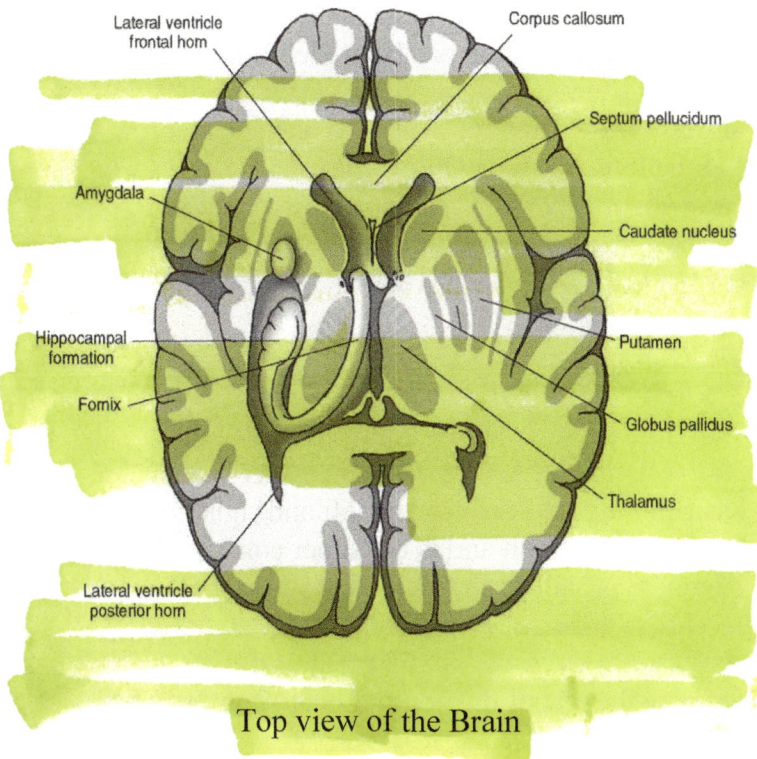

Top view of the Brain

GOD, THE BRAIN, THE BIBLE AND YOUR BODY

Inside the brain exists the pia mater meaning tender mother and the dura mater meaning hard mother. They are separated by the arachnoid mater, which circulates the CSF in the subarachnoid space (between the arachnoid and pia mater). The CSF bathes the central nervous system and descends down into the sacrum where it must be raised back up to the optic thalamus and pineal gland to be "reenergized". The four rivers are also symbolic for the four circulatory systems. Red blood is the Hiddekel River, Cerebral spinal fluid is the Euphrates River, urine is Pishon or Uizhun known locally as the golden river aka Piss for Pishon. The Gihon river is described as "winding through the entire land of Cush", which is associated with Ethiopia. For this reason, the Gihon has been identified as the Nile River. In addition to the four rivers, the body has four brains. These four are identified as the Cerebrum, Cerebellum, Medulla Oblongata, and Solar Plexus. The cerebellum is heart shaped and called the heart in Greek — thus "As a man thinketh in his heart so is he. (Proverbs 23.7)

Which brings us to Genesis again, beginning in chapter 11: And Abram and Nahor took them wives: the name of Abram's wife was **Sarai**; this is the cerebrum for the names Sarai and Abram combined is cerebrum and basically means to cover, the left and right portions of the top of the brain and is the super conscientious. Abraham is called the father of the Jews because the cerebrum is the father of the body. In embryology, the cerebrum is the first organ formed and is responsible for forming the rest of the body. Located on the outermost

GOD, THE BRAIN, THE BIBLE AND YOUR BODY

layer of the cerebrum is the Cerebral cortex made of copper and the pineal gland made of carbon. This is what produces electricity in the body. Again, I refer to the bible. And he made two cherubims of gold, beaten out of one piece made he them, on the two ends of the mercy seat; 8 One cherub on the end on this side, and another cherub on the other end on that side: out of the mercy seat made he the cherubims on the two ends thereof. 9 And the cherubims spread out their wings on high, and covered with their wings over the mercy seat, with their faces one to another; even to the mercy seatward were the faces of the cherubims. (Exod. 37.7) Here we see two cherubims, which is the same word as Cerebrum; additionally the wings of the cherubims cover the mercy seat or vail, in the same fashion that the dura mater and pia mater are covered by the arachnoid mater. This description of the Ark of the Covenant is similar to the way the pituitary and pineal glands are in the brain along with the sphenoid bone, which resembles the cherubim. And when they came to Nachon's threshing floor, Uzzah put forth his hand to the ark of God, and took hold of it; for the oxen shook it. 7 And the anger of the LORD was kindled against Uzzah; and God smote him there for his error; and there he died by the ark of God. (2 Sam 6.6) Some have suggested God electrocuted Uzzah, and using that theory, we see how the body produces electricity via the cerebral cortex, thalamus and the pineal gland. Under the inner cerebrum is the colostrum, sometimes called the Holy colostrum because it secretes a fluid, the cerebral spinal fluid (CSF). Secretion and secret are the same word. The CSF goes through the pineal gland and pituitary gland to differentiate into an electrical force. There are three energy centers, which go down the spinal column, and they are the spinal cord, the pin gala and the Ida. The pin gala comes from the pineal gland and is electric and masculine and it goes down the spinal cord. Eastern religions refer to the pin gala as the kundalini. The Ida is its counterpart and called the kundabuffer.

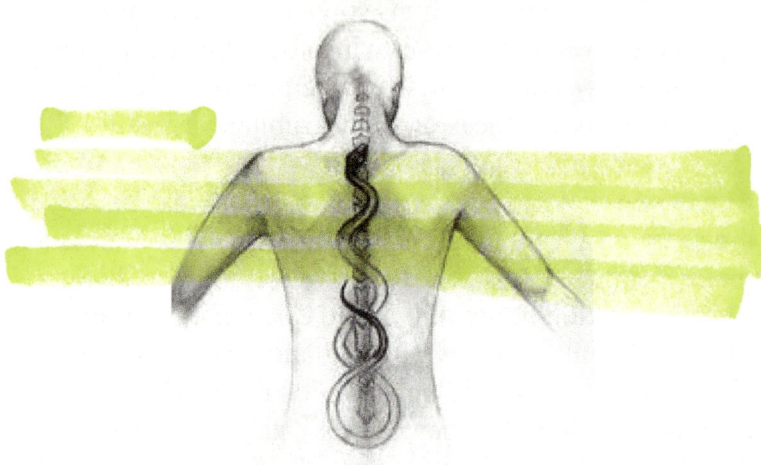

Kundalini

On the other side is the pituitary gland, it is feminine and it is the Sarah, Mary, Aset principle. Combined these two present duality and balance as Asar and Aset, Abraham and Sarah, Joseph and Mary. They become the honey and the milk because they secrete honey and milk, respectively. The pituitary gives magnetic energy and travels down the spin to the sacrum or sacral chakra, the second bottom chakra, below the solar plexus known as the place of the sun. Sacral is the word secret and secretion. According to German physician, neurologist Johann C. Reil's; the claustrum is a thin sheet of isolated gray matter, found just medial to the island of Reil. It is a sheet of peculiar gray substance and is made up of fusiform (spindle shaped) cell-bodies. "It is from this claustrum that contains yellow substance within its outer grayer exterior, that the wonderful, priceless oil is formed that flows down into the olivary fasciculus or olivospinal tract, 'descending with the rubrospinal tract through the reticular formation in the pons and medulla to the lateral corticospinal track of the spinal cord. It terminates in the gray matter of the spinal cord, probably giving off collaterals to corresponding nuclei in the brain stem. "santee, this is the oil, the precious gift of which the bible speaks, "thou anointest my head with oil." Thou preparest a table before me in the presence of mine enemies: thou anointest my head with oil; my cup runneth over. (Psalms 23.5)

What happens in the body is this fluid reaches the pons and the medulla oblongata, which again is one of the four brains of the human being. When it arrives there, it crosses the vagus or pneumo-gastric nerve: pneumo meaning air or the lungs and gastric is the stomach. Therefore, this nerve supplies the stomach and the lungs. The vagus nerve resembles a tree and crosses at the top of the spine. These nerves come from the pineal gland and the pituitary gland in one of the four rivers or chambers called the four ventricles in the brain. Between those two glands is the optic thalamus or thalamus a Greek word-meaning chamber. This

GOD, THE BRAIN, THE BIBLE AND YOUR BODY

chamber is equivalent to the Kings chamber in the great pyramid.

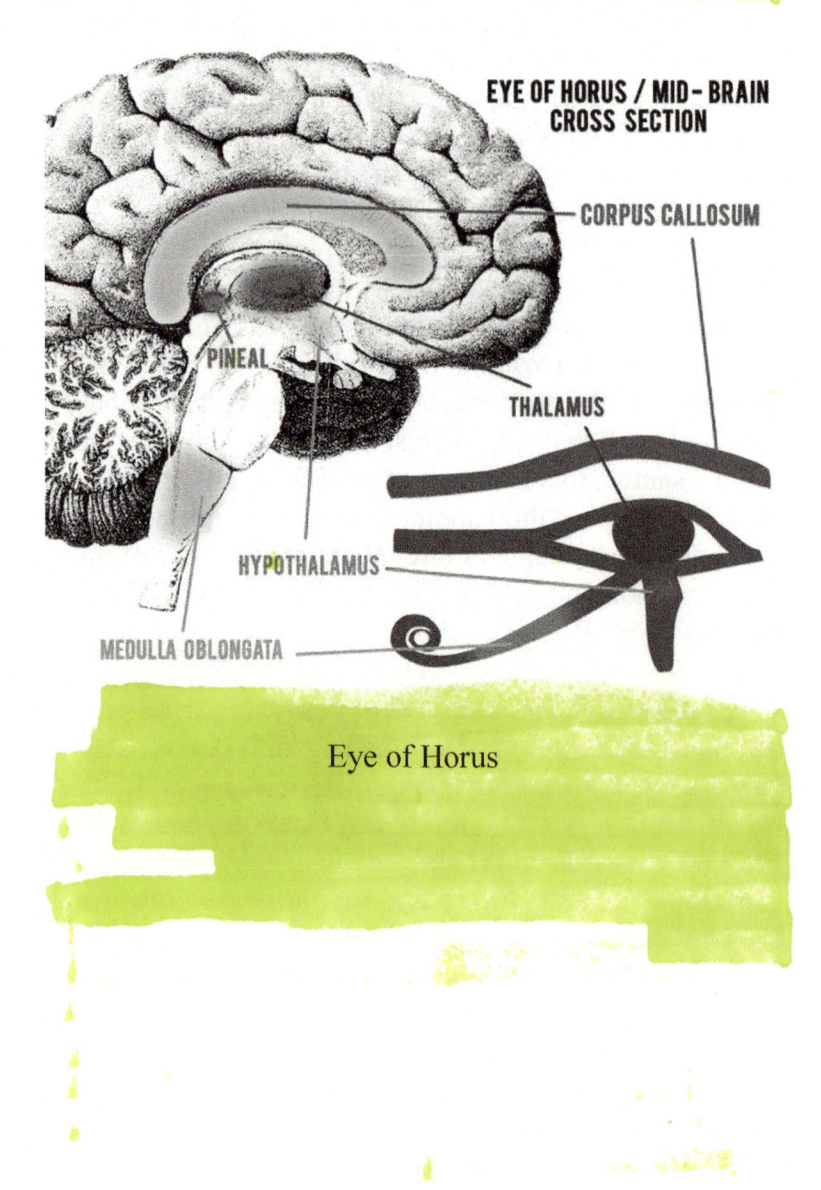

EYE OF HORUS / MID-BRAIN CROSS SECTION

- CORPUS CALLOSUM
- PINEAL
- THALAMUS
- HYPOTHALAMUS
- MEDULLA OBLONGATA

Eye of Horus

GOD, THE BRAIN, THE BIBLE AND YOUR BODY

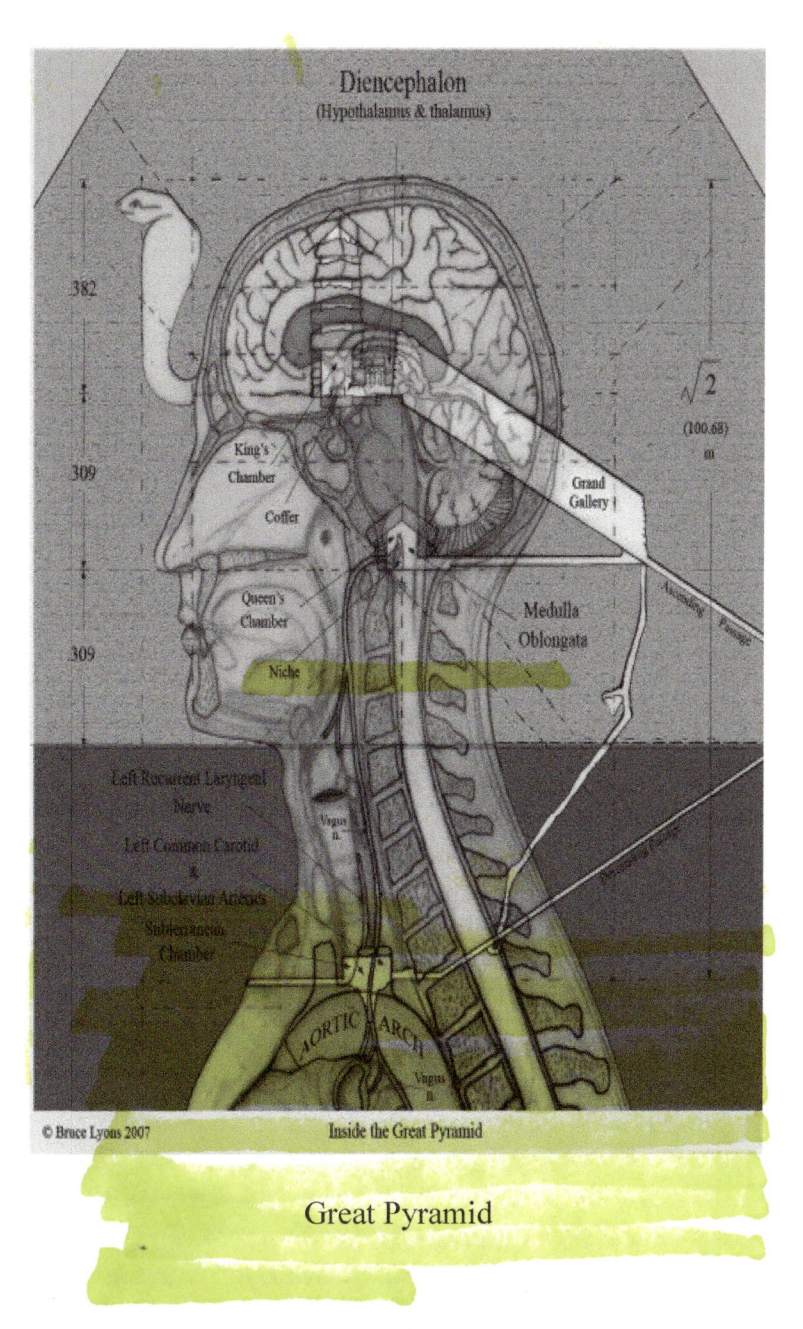

Inside the Great Pyramid
© Bruce Lyons 2007

Great Pyramid

GOD, THE BRAIN, THE BIBLE AND YOUR BODY

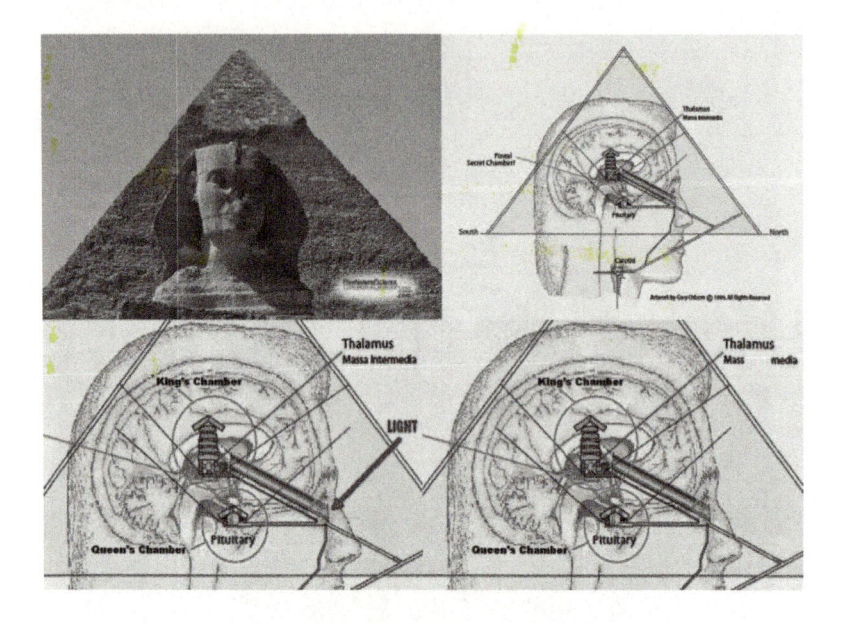

Kings/Queens Chamber

This front face view of the great pyramid shows how the Har em Akhet (Sphinx) is aligned so that the thalamus and pineal gland aligns with the king's chamber and the pituitary gland is located where the Queens chamber is constructed. Furthermore, the king's chamber aligns to the star system Orion originally called Sahu and the queen's chamber points to the Sirius star system originally called Sopdet. The ancient Egyptians related the deity Osiris originally known as Wsir or Asar to Orion and Aset misnomer Isis to the star called Sirius. When one looks at the word Osiris, it can be broken down as Os a medical word meaning opening and Iris, the thin circular structure in the eye. Thus, the word Osiris should be translated as Opening of the Eye. The eye they are referring to is the "Third Eye" which is located where the Pineal gland and optic thalamus are located. It leaves little doubt the ancient Egyptians knew God resides in the head. They taught the Greeks this same knowledge and this is why later European drawings showed God as inhabiting the brain/mind. According to Manly P. Hall's Secret Teaching of All Ages. (Photo: Egyptian Museum, Turin, Italy) EA Wallis Burge has noted that in the papyrus illustrating the entrance of the souls of the dead into the judgment hall of Osiris the deceased person has a pinecone attached to the crown of his head. Thyrsus of Baccus (pineal gland aka pine cone) and corresponds to the third eye of the Cyclops.

Pine cone/Cobras

GOD, THE BRAIN, THE BIBLE AND YOUR BODY

As you view this image, you notice the pinecone attached to a staff and two winding snakes surround the staff, similar to the way the spine is encompassed by the kundalini and is attached to the pineal gland, of another note this is the origin of the medical symbol called caduceus. The great pyramid contains four shafts. These four shafts point to the stars Thuban in Draco, Al Nitak in Orion, Sirius located in Canis Major and Kawkab (meaning the star in Arabic found in Usra Minor) the airshaft on the right points to Thuban, which was the pole star roughly 5,000 years ago. A pole star is a point around which the heavens appear to turn and it is normally the star closest to the north celestial pole, hence the name pole star. Thuban is Arabic for snake because it is a part of the constellation, Draco the dragon. This is but one reason you find the snake on the namuz (headdress) of pharaohs. The snake was secretly "worshipped" by the priest while the rest of the world acknowledged the bull during the age of Ptah and Osiris presently called the Age of Taurus. They are opposing forces in the zodiac and six months apart. Notice these four shafts relate to the biblical story of the Garden in Eden beginning with God (Kawkab – Usra Minor), Adam (Orion – al Nitak), Eve (Sirius – Canis Major), and the snake (Thuban – Draco). Another example of how the genesis story is told in the great pyramid shafts is that one of the shafts point to Orion. Orion is Adam or Atom (Atum) who had a rib removed from him to make Eve according to Genesis And the LORD God caused a deep sleep to fall upon Adam and he slept: and he took one of his ribs, and closed up the flesh instead thereof; 22 And the rib, which the LORD God had taken from

42

man, made he a woman, and brought her unto the man. 23 And Adam said, This is now bone of my bones, and flesh of my flesh: she shall be called Woman, because she was taken out of Man. (Gen. 2:21) This is the process of splitting atoms. Atoms are neutral; they contain the same number of protons as electrons. However, when an electron is removed from an atom it becomes an ion and begins to change. By definition, an ion is an electrically charged particle produced by either removing electrons from a neutral atom to give a positive ion or adding electrons to a neutral atom to give a negative ion. Thus, God removed a rib or electron from the atom or Adam to multiply it. So now, when you look at the word Orion (Or-ion) you see how Egyptian science of splitting atoms is incorporated into the bible using symbolism.

The Sistine chapel was named after Pope Sixtus IV who restored it from 1477-1480. It is the official residence of the Pope in Vatican City. Inside of the Sistine Chapel is a mural of the creation of Adam by Michelangelo who was commissioned by Pope Julius II in 1508. What Michelangelo came up with has been hidden from the masses of Christians who view this work. It is actually a picture of God inside a human brain.

Sistine Chapel

GOD, THE BRAIN, THE BIBLE AND YOUR BODY

Sistine Chapel

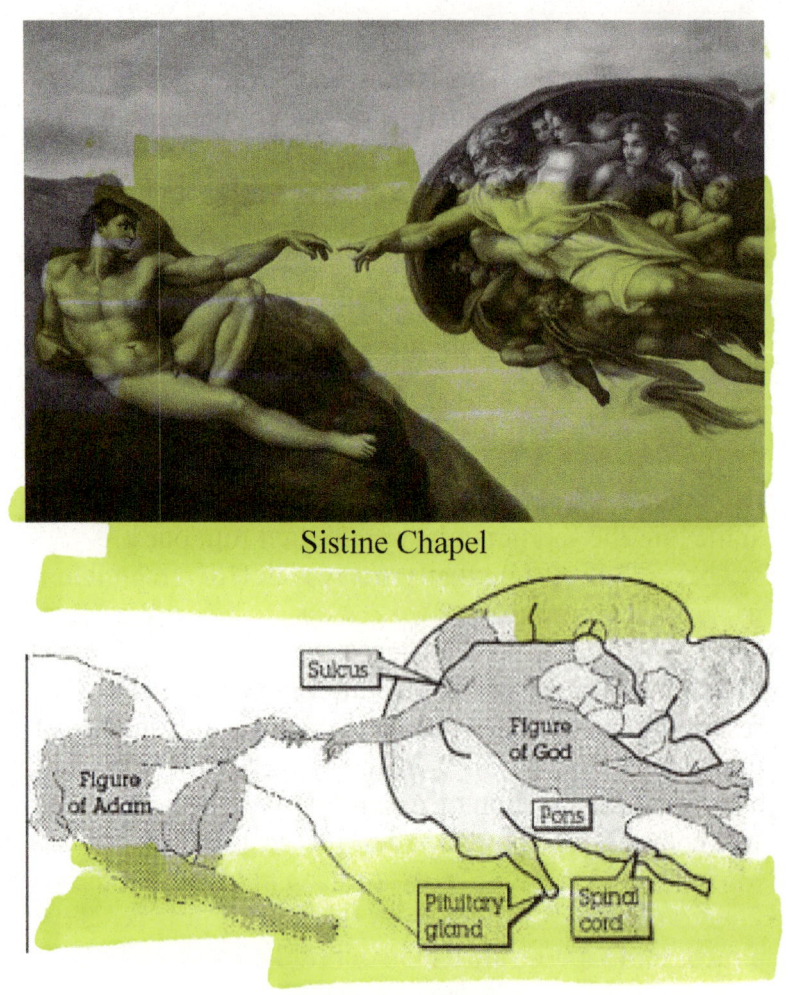

God/Adam/Brain

As we continue with the CSF, metaphysically, we learn when the oil rises and passes the pneumo-gastric nerve; it is "crucified" in the head. This is why the bible teaches Jesus was crucified at Golgotha a Hebrew word meaning Skull as well as Mt. Calvary is a Latin word

GOD, THE BRAIN, THE BIBLE AND YOUR BODY

meaning head/skull. Thus, the crucifixion had to happen because unless Jesus is crucified, he cannot save the "world". Similarly, you cannot be saved unless you are also crucified and the oil touches the optic thalamus. And he that taketh not his cross, and followeth after me, is not worthy of me. (Matt. 10.38) The thalamus resembles an egg and was called "the light of the world". Thus Jesus said, "I'm the light of the world". As well as the light of the body is the eye: therefore when thine eye is single, thy whole body also is full of light; but when thine eye is evil, thy body also is full of darkness. (Luke 11.34) The oil must travel from the head or heaven, where God is, and down the spine into the sacrum to be returned. From our biblical studies, we are taught that Jesus was in Heaven and sent down to earth to be crucified and to return to God. For I came down from heaven, not to do mine own will, but the will of him that sent me. (John 6. 38) Therefore, we must also follow this path, not a literal path of crucifixion but a metaphysical/spiritual path of crucifying the oil. This happens inside the body. There are five sections of the spine/vertebrae numbered together are 33 the exact age Jesus was at death. Thirty-three (33) separate bones form the spine. These include seven cervical vertebrae, 12 thoracic vertebrae, five lumbar vertebrae, one sacrum (5 fused vertebrae) and one coccyx (4 fused vertebrae).

GOD, THE BRAIN, THE BIBLE AND YOUR BODY

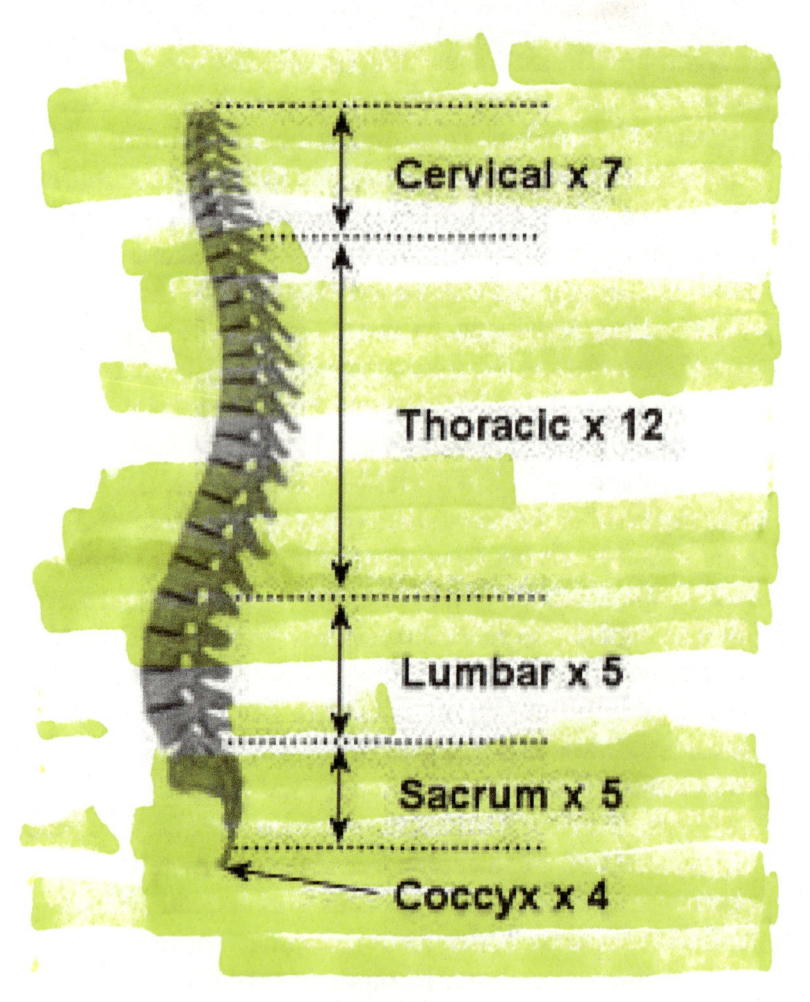

Cervical x 7

Thoracic x 12

Lumbar x 5

Sacrum x 5

Coccyx x 4

33 Vertebrae

GOD, THE BRAIN, THE BIBLE AND YOUR BODY

According to the online etymology dictionary, the sacrum is defined as **sacrum (n.)**
> bone at the base of the spine, 1753, from Late Latin *os sacrum* "sacred bone,"

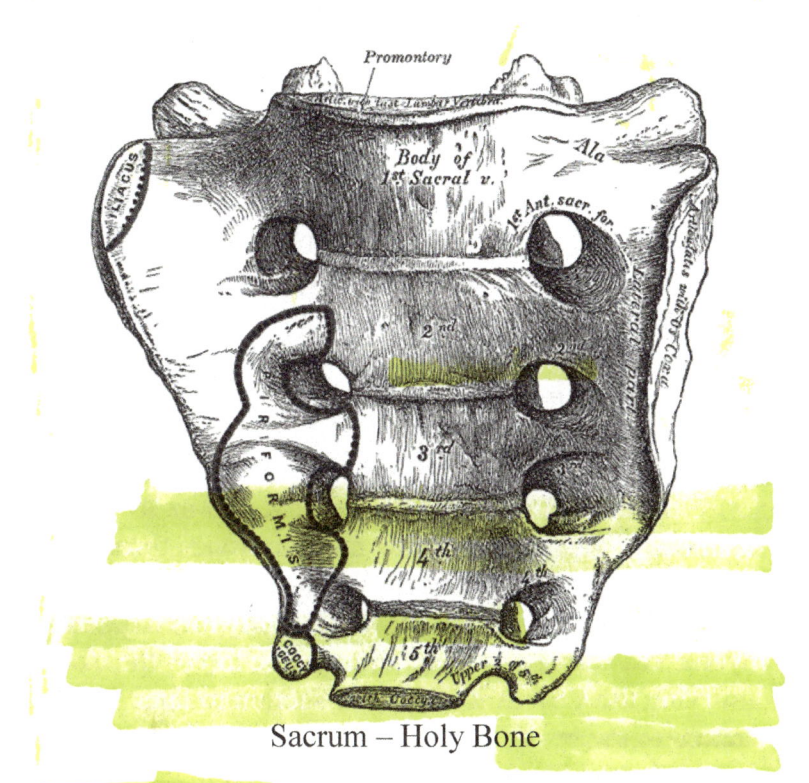

Sacrum – Holy Bone

At birth, the sacrum starts as five separate bones but around age 16-18, they fuse to become one bone around the area where the kundalini lies at the base of the spine. This sacrum shows up symbolically in the bible as the stones Jacob rested on as well as the stones David used to slay the giant Goliath. And he lighted upon a certain place, and tarried there all night, because the sun was set;

GOD, THE BRAIN, THE BIBLE AND YOUR BODY

and he took of the stones of that place, and put them for his pillows, and lay down in that place to sleep. 12 And he dreamed, and behold a ladder set up on the earth, and the top of it reached to heaven: and behold the angels of God ascending and descending on it. 13 And, behold, the LORD stood above it, and said, I am the LORD God of Abraham thy father, and the God of Isaac: the land whereon thou liest, to thee will I give it, and to thy seed; 16 And Jacob awaked out of his sleep, and he said, Surely the LORD is in this place; and I knew it not. 17 And he was afraid, and said, How dreadful is this place! This is none other but the house of God, and this is the gate of heaven. 18 And Jacob rose up early in the morning, and took the stone that he had put for his pillows, and set it up for a pillar, and poured oil upon the top of it. (Gen. 28.11-18)

Notice in verse 11 he took stones plural, but in 18 it became a single stone meaning the five stones fused, together just as the five bones begin to fuse together in the human body at age 16-18, coincidently this happens in verse 18! He also poured oil upon the top of the stone signifying the CSF as it bathes the sacrum to later be returned to the brain. Later we see And David girded his sword upon his armour, and he assayed to go; for he had not proved it. And David said unto Saul, I cannot go with these; for I have not proved them. And David put them off him. 40 And he took his staff in his hand, and chose him five smooth stones out of the brook, and put them in a shepherd's bag, which he had, even in a scrip; and his sling was in his hand: and he drew near to the Philistine. (1 Sam. 17.39) This is symbolism of man slaying the giant: his lower nature that feeds off lust, greed and all things anti-God. Thus when you are crucified you raise your vibration or higher self and become one again with God. Another way it is said is "Rob Peter to pay Paul". Peter means rock; Peter is derived from the Greek word *Πετρος (Petros)* meaning "stone". You will also find the word *Cephas*, meaning "stone" in Aramaic (Refer to Matthew 16:18 and John 1:42). This "rock" is the sacred plexus or sacrum, whereas Paul is in the head, ruled by the planet Saturn. Therefore, when you rob Peter to pay Paul, you're overindulging in sinful actions. Therefore, Jacob wrestling with his lower nature overpowered the angel and was called Israel, meaning Ascend to God. He raised the oil and it ascends back into the pineal gland and thalamus area. Hence, Jacob called that place Peniel that is Pineal. And Jacob called the name of the place Peniel: for I have seen God face to face and my life is preserved. (Gen 32.30) Pineal is the pine cone shaped gland found in the middle of our brain. The pineal gland is also called the epiphysis cerebri. Epiphysis is related to the word Epiphany a word meaning the manifestation of God and is celebrated annually on January 6. The Pineal gland secretes melatonin; melatonin secretes a hormone named serotonin which is a neurotransmitter found primarily in our gastrointestinal tract. Another name for the pineal gland is the parietal eye which the American Heritage Medical dictionary defines as a photo sensory organ located on the top of the head of certain reptiles, chiefly lizards. Also called *pineal eye, third eye*. The melatonin is secreted from the pineal gland only by the absence of light. Biblically this is supported The

GOD, THE BRAIN, THE BIBLE AND YOUR BODY

light of the body is the eye: if therefore thine eye be single, thy whole body shall be full of light. (Matt. 6.22)

Atlas

This story is symbolically told in the ancient story of Atlas who holds the world on his shoulder. Physiologically, in the spinal column the first vertebrae is called atlas and it is responsible or holding or attaching the head to the body.

From Jacob later called Israel came the 12 tribes of Israel, the 12 tribes are symbolically the 12 cranial nerves in the head, the 12 cranial nerves serve as the 12 signs of the zodiac and the 12 gems of the breastplate where the 12 nerves in the solar plexus are covered. And Joshua set up twelve stones in the midst of Jordan, in the place where the feet of the priests which bare the Ark of the Covenant stood: and they are there unto this day (Josh. 4.9)

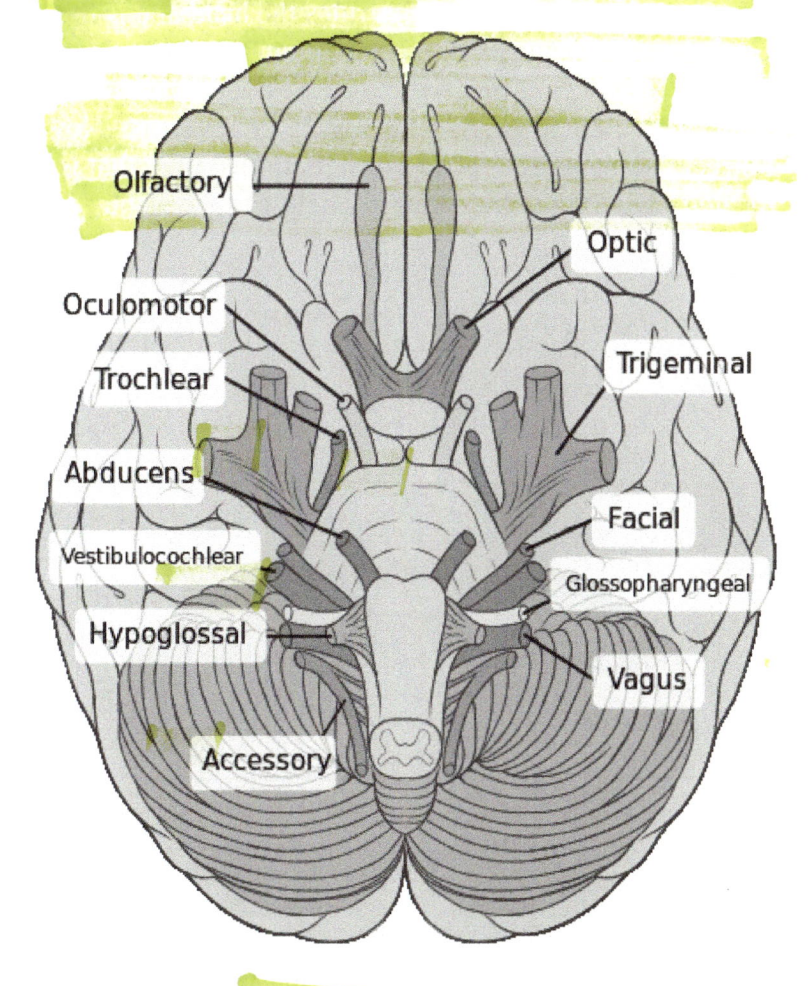

Twelve Cranial Nerves

GOD, THE BRAIN, THE BIBLE AND YOUR BODY

Each cranial nerve is symbolic of a star constellation along the ecliptic, just as the different parts inside the brain relate to a star constellation. As mentioned earlier, the Thalamus is the kings chamber and points to Orion, the queens chamber is the pituitary and points to Sirius. Here are other examples, Aries rules the head and is the cerebrum, and Taurus is the cerebellum. Refer to figure called Constellation and it shows the Fornix, which is adjacent to the thalamus in the middle of the brain. Now I direct your attention to the constellation Fornax that is located adjacent to Orion slightly below to the right.

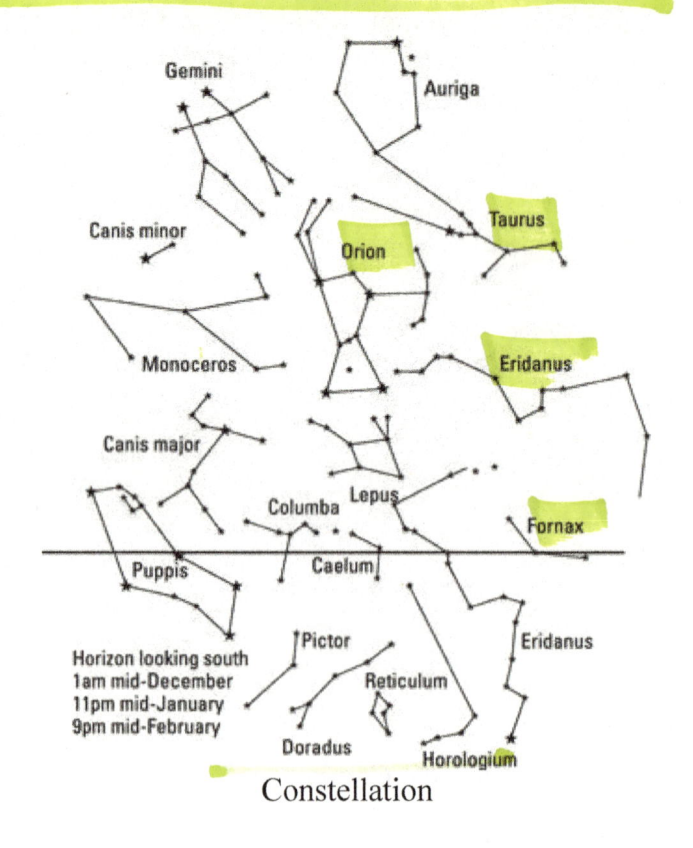

Constellation

GOD, THE BRAIN, THE BIBLE AND YOUR BODY

Directly above Fornax is Eridanus or the Jordanus (Jordan) river in Taurus coming from the foot of Orion and is the ventricular system in the head, which relates back to the four rivers of the brain. This is the Land of milk and honey as the Milky Way runs between Taurus and Gemini. Matthew 3:13 tells us Jesus was baptized by John the Baptist in the river Jordan. This river "baptizes" the inner brain where Christ is located.

Another constellation is Auriga and according to mythology, it represented the scimitar or crook. The crook of Auriga represents someone who is a goat herder or shepherd – Jesus was called the Good shepherd. The Auriga constellation was associated with the oratory system in the lower head and neck called the auricular nerve that runs right behind the ear and down the neck. Slightly below the nasal bone is the foramen ovale or For Amen. Amen is Amun and means the hidden one which refers to Jesus And unto the angel of the church of the Laodiceans write; These things saith the Amen, the faithful and true witness, the beginning of the creation of God. (Rev. 3.14) Another more familiar name is the hippocampus from the Greek words *hippocampus* from Greek: ἵππος, "horse" and κάμπος, "sea monster") because it resembles a sea horse.

GOD, THE BRAIN, THE BIBLE AND YOUR BODY

Hippocampus/Sea Horse

There is a part of our brain called the horn of Ammon. Danish anatomist Jacob Winslow has called this Ammon's horn. It is a group of nerve cells within the hippocampus, which are clustered together in the shape of a horn, and make up the 'horn of Ammon'. "The hippocampus consists of two 'horns' that curve back from the area of the hypothalamus to the amygdala.

GOD, THE BRAIN, THE BIBLE AND YOUR BODY

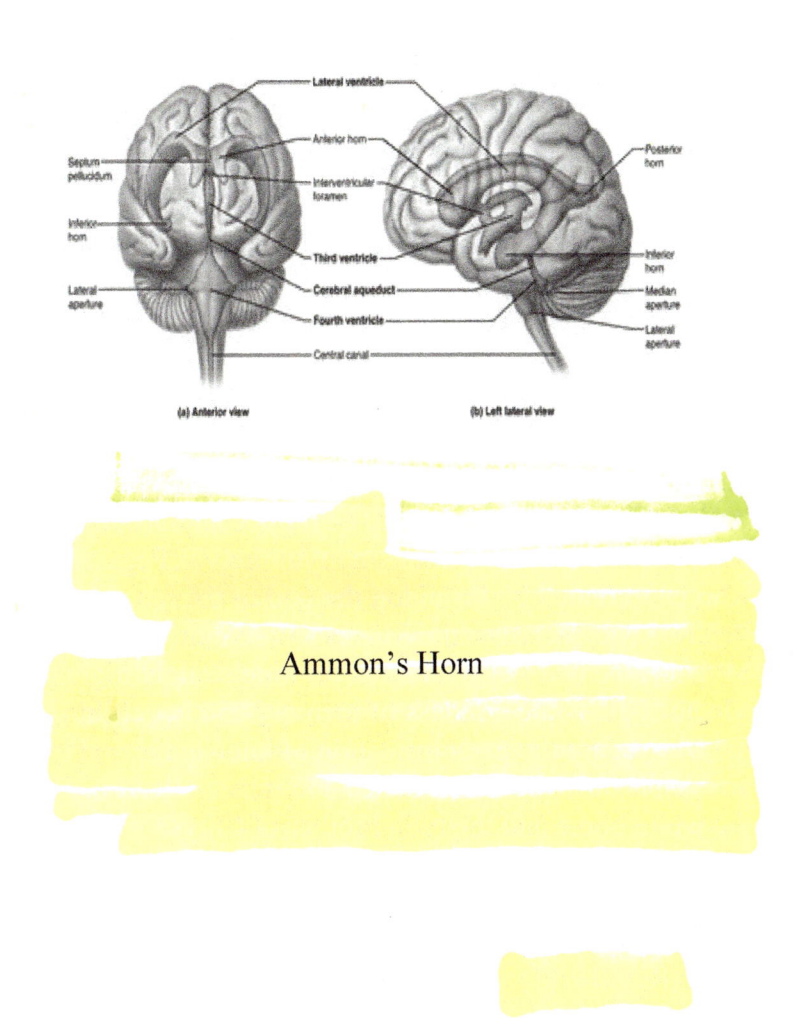

Ammon's Horn

GOD, THE BRAIN, THE BIBLE AND YOUR BODY

Amun

Ammon's horn was symbolized in ancient Egypt as Amun the ram headed deity. The hippocampus deals with memory. The sea horse in mythology is Pegasus who was created by Poseidon the god of the sea. Pegasus was sacred to the Muses whose mother Mnemosyne had sex with Zeus for nine straight nights. Mnemosyne is the goddess of memory and her children, the Muses, are the personification of knowledge and the arts, especially literature, dance and music. Pegasus is the white horse and the twin brother of Chrysaor (Chrysler). And I saw heaven opened, and behold a white horse; and he that sat upon him was called Faithful and True, and in righteousness he doth judge and make war. (Rev. 19.11)

He was associated with the southern band of constellations called the stars of Ea, and also with the

GOD, THE BRAIN, THE BIBLE AND YOUR BODY

constellation AŠ-IKU, the Field or the square of Pegasus. This is further proof of the association of the cosmology and the gods. In the story of Zoroaster it is written a white horse straddled him as a child to protect him from harm which is the same way the hippocampus of the brain straddles the pineal gland. In the Quran of the Muslims in Surah Al Isra, Muhammad also rides a white horse/donkey called Al Buraq a word meaning lightning. Interesting that Al Isra is an anagram for Israel (Isra Al). Therefore, the hero riding a white horse is symbolism for the region of the brain called the hippocampus. It was taken from mythological writings of the ancients to express the inner workings of the brain and how the optic thalamus and pineal gland is the Son/Sun and/or hero. In today's time, the movie industry shows you the knight and the horse, another name for a young female horse is a mare, which gives you the word nightmare. For those that recall the Lone Ranger rode a white mare named Dusty before acquiring the white horse called silver. Physiologically, dreams deal with memories thus the reader should be able to make the connection between the hippocampus, mares and knights.

Inside the brain attached to the end of the hippocampus is the amygdala. The amygdala comes from the Latin word amygdalum meaning almond, as it resembles an almond. It was also called in the Arabic language Al-Lauzatani meaning the two tonsils or literally the two almonds. This word is almost identical to the word Magdalene. Magdalene refers to Mary one of the secret disciples of Jesus. Madgalene has been defined as

GOD, THE BRAIN, THE BIBLE AND YOUR BODY

follows. Madgdalene fem. Proper name, from Latin (Maria) Magdalena, from Greek Magdalene, literally "woman of Magdala," from Aramaic (Semetic) Maghdela, place on the Sea of Galilee, literally "tower." In Hebrew *Migdal* means "tower", "fortress"; in Aramaic, "Magdala" means "tower" or "elevated, great, magnificent"

Mary Magdalene

GOD, THE BRAIN, THE BIBLE AND YOUR BODY

The amygdala has two sections, one called the anterior amygdala and the other the posterior amygdala. The amygdala deals with our emotions, such as fear, anger and pleasure. It is also responsible for what memories will be stored in our minds. It receives sensory information from the thalamus and from the cerebral cortex. The posterior amygdala deals with traumas and dramas of life. Alternatively, the anterior amygdala brings euphoria. You can reach this euphoric state by inhaling scents or hearing certain sounds and vibrations. These stimulate the neurons of the amygdala to open to higher spiritual experiences This is why the bible speaks of oils used to annoint the body as well as burning of incense specifically frankinscence. Another way is the burning of essential oil. Essential oils are liquids that are distilled from plants, shrubs, flowers, trees, roots, bushes and seeds. Oils extracted from these life givers are the closest to human plasma that we have on this Earth. These oils can be applied all over the body but especially to the bottom of the feet where it takes only about 20 minutes for them to travel up the body. When the scents from the oils are inhaled, they carry neurons via the nose hairs and travel to the brain. This helps heals and cleanses the body of "sin". Therefore, the bible summarizes this brain function this way.

And, behold, a woman in the city, which was a sinner, when she knew that Jesus sat at meat in the Pharisee's house, brought an alabaster box of ointment, 38 And stood at his feet behind him weeping, and began to wash his feet with tears, and did wipe them with the hairs of her head, and kissed his feet, and anointed them with the

GOD, THE BRAIN, THE BIBLE AND YOUR BODY

ointment. 39 Now when the Pharisee which had bidden him saw it, he spake within himself, saying, This man, if he were a prophet, would have known who and what manner of woman this is that toucheth him: for she is a sinner. 40 And Jesus answering said unto him, Simon, I have somewhat to say unto thee. And he saith, Master, say on. 41 There was a certain creditor which had two debtors: the one owed five hundred pence, and the other fifty. 42 And when they had nothing to pay, he frankly forgave them both. Tell me therefore, which of them will love him most? 43 Simon answered and said, I suppose that he, to whom he forgave most. And he said unto him, Thou hast rightly judged. 44 And he turned to the woman, and said unto Simon, Seest thou this woman? I entered into thine house, thou gavest me no water for my feet: but she hath washed my feet with tears, and wiped them with the hairs of her head. 45 Thou gavest me no kiss: but this woman since the time I came in hath not ceased to kiss my feet. 46 My head with oil thou didst not anoint: but this woman hath anointed my feet with ointment. (Luke 3.37-46)

Again, the amygdala can produce euophoric feelings of lust and memories of sexual experiences, thus some in the Christian community called Mary Magdalene a prostitute. She has been venerated as well as demonized by the church. The earlier Anglican, Catholic and Eastern Orthodox churches venerated her by naming a day July 22 (7/22) after her. Some say the gospel of Luke allude to the woman with seven demons caste out of her as Mary Magdalene. This falls in line with the western churches perception of her. The dark sayings associated with this is interesting, as amygdala means almonds. Almonds throughout antiquity were regarded as fertility symbols. The aroma of almond supposedly arouses passion in females. Therefore, it comes as no surprise to the author that the symbol for Christianity the fish resembles the almond, as both are fertility symbols. The Vesica piscis is a shape formed when two circles intersect at their vertices. This shape is called the mandorla an Italian word-meaning almond.

Vesica Piscis

When the measurement of the vesica piscis is extracted the formula amounts to 153/256. Thus it is again a dark saying when we read in John the following quote. Simon Peter went up, and drew the net to land full of great fishes, and hundred and fifty and three: and for all there were so many, yet was not the net. (John 21.11)

GOD, THE BRAIN, THE BIBLE AND YOUR BODY

This 153 is the ratio of the vesica pisces or Ichthys as it was later called. It has a ratio of 153/256. In Greek gematria or numerology, her name Magdalene "η Μαγδαληνή" bears the number
8 + 40 + 1 + 3 + 4 + 1 + 30 + 8 + 50 + 8 = 153.
According to the Jewish encyclopedia, the Tetragrammaton is found 153 times in the Old Testament. One hundred fifty three (153) is a ratio of Pi, when you divide 22/7 you get 22/7 = 3.142857142857 or Pi. If the reader will recall Mary Magdalene day is July 22 or 22/7. The well-known but elusive Balm of Gilead is mentioned three times in the Bible (Genesis 37:25; Jeremiah 8:22; Jeremiah 46:11). It had near miraculous properties. Not only did it heal wounds, its aroma made men dizzy with lust. A woman had only to dab the oil on her heel to catch the nose of a man she fancied.

Lastly, the total number of men employed to work on Solomon's Temple is a total of 153,600 men. [17] And Solomon numbered all the strangers that were in the land of Israel, after the numbering wherewith David his father had numbered them; and they were found an hundred and fifty thousand and three thousand and six hundred. [18] And he set threescore and ten thousand of them to be bearers of burdens, and fourscore thousand to be hewers in the mountain, and three thousand and six hundred overseers to set the people a work. (2Chron. 2:2, 17-18) Therefore, this furthers hammers the author's point about the parts of the brain and how they are associated with the bible.

GOD, THE BRAIN, THE BIBLE AND YOUR BODY

Four Beasts

Hypothetical Correspondence Between Ancient Egyptian Cosmology and the Cranial Vault

The Vault of Heaven

Horus and the Sun Disk

Corpus Callosum (the barque)
Thalamus (Ra's sun disk)
Pineal (Osiris)
Pituitary (Isis)
Cerebral Peduncle, Pons, and Medulla Oblongata (Horus)
Brain Stem

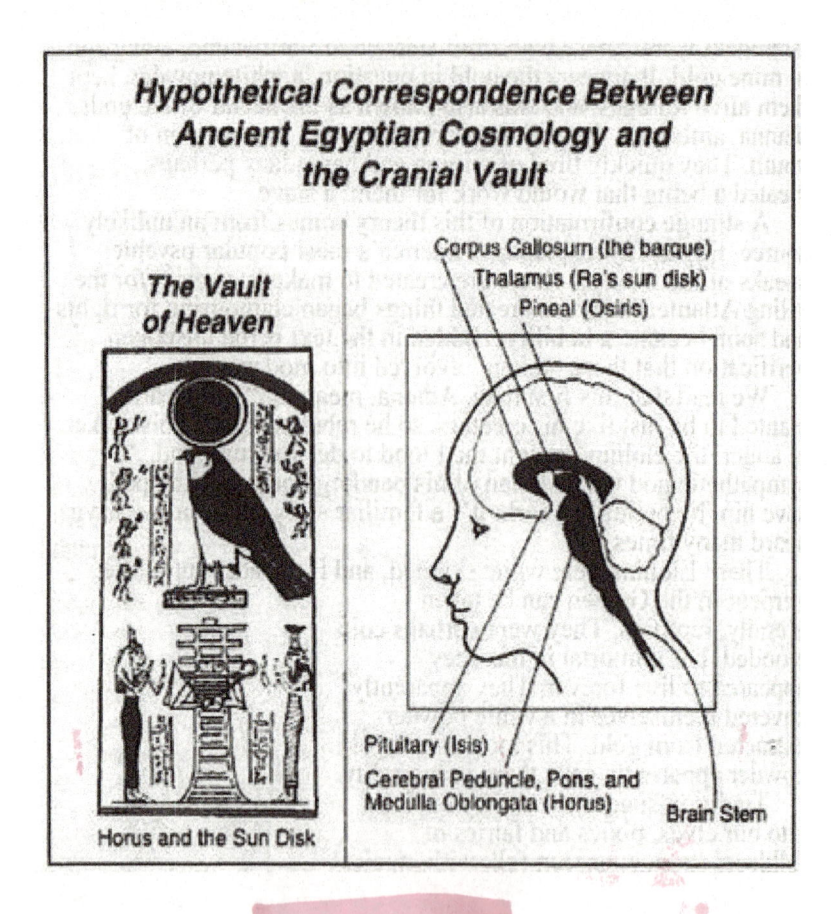

Egyptian Cosmology

All of this knowledge originated in Africa of course as they were the original acknowledgers of the sun. As the Sun rose in the east, they would face it and align their pineal gland, optic thalamus, third eye with the sun; this is now known as sun gazing. The health benefits of sun gazing include increased levels of the neurotransmitters, Serotonin and Melatonin, which improves the quality of sleep; it fights fatigue as well as boosts energy. Sun gazing is also known to increase the size of the pineal gland, improves endocrine health, lastly it improves dream recall, improves eyesight and is said to cure certain physical elements like cancer. NASA has studied this ancient practice called sun gazing or HRM phenomenon named after Hira Ratan Manek who gets his nutrients from the sun and does not eat. Biblically, sun gazing is found in the book of Ezekiel And he brought me into the inner court of the LORD's house, … toward the temple of the LORD, and their faces toward the east; and they worshipped the sun toward the east. (Ezek. 8.16) you also find references to turning towards the rising sun in Numbers 2:3 and Joshua 19:34. Sun gazing is an ancient practice as seen in this image from King Tut Ankh Amun's tomb. This relief is from ANTECHAMBER, North Wall (west to east) and is Utterance 302 458: To say the words: "Serene(?) is the sky, Soped lives (i.e., shines), for it is Unas indeed who is the living (star), the son of Sothis. As one sun gazes and get their nutrients from the sun, they in turn become a sun just as Unas was becoming the son of Sothis.

Sun Gazing

Even our great musician Stevie Wonder recognized this in his album cover for Innervisions. Star gazing can be dangerous if not properly regimented. The sun emits the lowest amount of ultra-violet radiation at dawn and sunset. Therefore, it is best to attempt sun gazing at these times. One should not attempt to gaze into the sun out of this window and for extended periods of time. Therefore, I warn the reader to not try this unless under the supervision of one who has mastered this ancient practice.

Religious Books are Sexual in Nature

The Bible and Quran and other religious texts are also sex books. In ancient Egypt, they had the Egyptian priest called Sem from where we get the words seminary and semen. The priests were representatives of Osiris who was shown as a tekhenu aka an obelisk (refer to the Washington monument) which are now seen as steeples in churches or as minarets in Islam. Minaret is named after the Egyptian deity Min who is shown holding an erect phallus in his hand. The dome is the breast. In religious architecture the dome proclaims the glory of God. The word dome comes from the Latin word domus meaning house from Italian duomo meaning a house of God aka the church. The word church comes from the word Kirke or Circe who was the sun goddess, daughter of Helios. This is where the word Circle originates. Also the word Domas is related to the word dynamite. Domas and domamas come from the word Yahweh which is the sex act because it represents the explosion of an orgasm. When churches give communion on the first Sunday, which consists of eating a wafer symbolic of the body of Christ and drinking wine/grape juice it represents the blood of Christ. This ritual comes from the Egyptians who practice a ritual form of cannibalism (Cain/Abel) when they would eat the bread and drink beer both made from wheat. According to an Egyptian temple they show grain growing out of the body of the dead Osiris while Isis soul hovers above the stalk. Isis is the one who transformed the god. Therefore, she reconstructed his body and fans life into him via her wings. Metaphorically, she becomes the divine baker who transforms raw grain into risen and nourishing bread. Thus, when a woman eats of the nourishing bread aka takes in his life essence she transforms this energy within her body.

The first commandment told to Adam and Eve in the bible was be fruitful and multiply. The first surah (Arabic word for chapter) in the Quran is suratul Alaq and it is the congealed blood or clot, a reference to sperm. The first chapter in the bible is Genesis or the generative principle. Then you have the testaments. The root word in testament is testes aka the scrotum located around the sacrum or holy bone. Testes also means skull and comes from the Late Latin word testa meaning a skull. This should allow you to see where the word tubal Cain comes from. When you are angry you raise cane (hell = lower chakras) but looking at it from this sexual perspective; raising Cain can also mean getting an erection. His brother's name is Abel meaning breath and also vanity. Astrologically, Abel is Aries and Cain is Taurus. The second Adam, Noah, was given the same commandment; be fruitful and multiply. The bible has an interesting story where Leah gave her mandrakes aka aphrodisiacs to Rachel and Rachel in exchange allowed Leah to have sex with Jacob. And Reuben went in the days of wheat harvest, and found mandrakes in the field, and brought them unto his mother Leah. Then Rachel said to Leah, Give me, I pray thee, of thy son's mandrakes. 15 And she said unto her, Is it a small matter that thou hast taken my husband? and wouldest thou take away my son's mandrakes also? And Rachel said, Therefore he shall lie with thee to night for thy son's

GOD, THE BRAIN, THE BIBLE AND YOUR BODY

mandrakes. 16 And Jacob came out of the field in the evening, and Leah went out to meet him, and said, Thou must come in unto me; for surely I have hired thee with my son's mandrakes. And he lay with her that night. 17 And God hearkened unto Leah, and she conceived, and bare Jacob the fifth son. (Gen. 30.14-17) She in essence sold drugs in exchange for sex. However, the author wants to talk about sex from a different perspective and that perspective is from a higher, spiritual concept.

When a man has sex with a woman, he leaves either his life force (semen) in her sacrum (pubic area) or her throat area via fellatio. The sex act is the transference of energy from the man to the woman also seen in the Kosmos as electricity converting to magnetism. Men, have you ever experienced being sleepy, drained or lack of energy and fatigue after sexual intimacy? When a man does not release his sperm, he retains the energy. Yet if he releases the energy in or on the woman, she gets the energy. Hence, most men will feel drained after sex while the woman is active. When she orgasms the chi (ki, prana, mana) energy is reabsorbed into her body thus she retains the energy force as opposed to transferring it. This is why it was considered a sin to spill your seed on the ground as Onan did. Onan was a descendant of Judah who did not want to impregnate his late brother's wife so when he began to orgasm he pulled out and spilled his seed. And Judah said unto Onan, Go in unto thy brother's wife, and marry her, and raise up seed to thy brother. 9 And Onan knew that the seed should not be his; and it came to pass, when he went in unto his brother's wife, that he spilled it on the ground, lest that

GOD, THE BRAIN, THE BIBLE AND YOUR BODY

he should give seed to his brother. (Gen. 38.8) When men refrain from sex and spilling their seed, they become physically strong, and growing up in the south, men that were not sexually active were called "cock strong". The association with the male rooster also known as a cockerel is that it rises in the morning along with the sun, just as the phallus rises in the morning.

Every month when the moon is in your sun sign, you are supposed to refrain from sex. When you do, you return a 10th back to god who resides in heaven (head). A tenth is ATEN or a 10. The phallic is the 1 and the circle is the O yoni. This is used for regeneration and is used to create or generate power. It's the sex act hidden in plain sight in electronics as the power symbol. Which when pushed brings things to life. You will eventually return to God because the semen with the life force comes from the brain down to the sacrum and then back up to the brain again. This is called tithing.

O	1	ϕ
Nothing	Unity / God	Nothing split by Unity is Phi, the constant of creation

Power Button

This is also the letter Q and signifies the moment of conception. Science has now admitted that light is emitted at the time of conception.
http://www.foxnews.com/health/2016/04/26/scientists-witness-flash-light-during-conception-say-discovery-could-aid-ivf.html

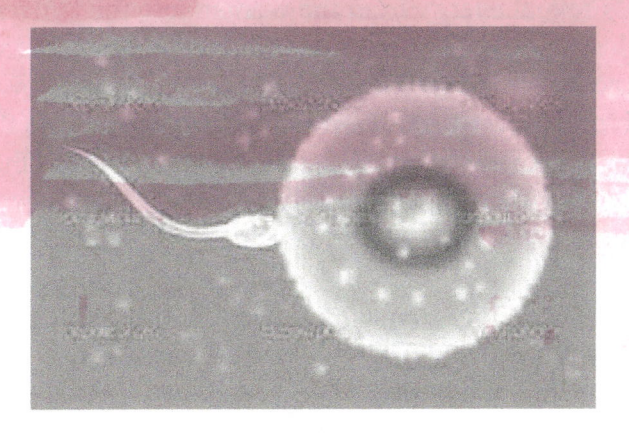

Fertilized Egg

Briefly, the reader should understand the English alphabet is also esoteric and encompasses hidden meanings. The first four letters of the alphabet ABCD mean Abra Cadabra representing the opening. As you travel down the alphabet you get to QRST, which phonetically is Christ, yet it is hidden and the hidden one is Amen/Amun, refer to Revelations 3:14.

The orgasmic feelings are caused by the aroused and expanding chi energy being generated and released. This stimulates the physical nerve-endings of the genital region and creates the euphoric feeling men have when

GOD, THE BRAIN, THE BIBLE AND YOUR BODY

having an orgasm. His release means that the vital chi energy is being transferred to the woman. Frequent sex is very taxing on the chi energy as well as the physical body this is why most religions teach to abstain from sexual relations. For women the process is similar albeit different. Women loose energy during menstruation as it expels sexual energy from the woman into the Universe. The lost eggs, uterine lining and blood are abundant with chi energy. It is said that 40% of our daily energy, we receive from food, air, water and sunlight goes into the production of sexual energy, which is then used in the production of sperm for males or the cultivation of eggs for the female.

The sexual energy is again produced in the sacral region of the body where the base chakra resides. This is where the kundalini, a feminine energy, originates and is called the coiled serpent. It is associated with the Ida and pin gala energy inside the body. The Ida is from the pituitary gland and is the feminine portion and the pin gala is from the pineal and is the masculine portion, joined by the shushumna the backbone or spine.

GOD, THE BRAIN, THE BIBLE AND YOUR BODY

Pingala Ida

These are called Nadis, which essentially means flow like a pipe, or tube that allows the flow of water/energy etc. and according to the tantras there are 72,000 or more such channels or networks through which the stimuli flows like an electric current from one point to another. They run along the spine through a series of energy seats called Chakras. (chakras will be discussed in more detail). And I saw in the right hand of him that sat on the throne a book written within and on the backside, sealed with seven seals. (Rev. 5.1) There are seven chakras within the human body. Of the seven, four are in the trunk of the body, two in the head and is one in the neck. The Kundalini lies coiled in three and a half coils, in a dormant or sleeping state. This is symbolized in the book of revelations. And I will give power unto my two witnesses, and they shall prophesy a thousand two hundred and threescore days, clothed in sackcloth. (Rev. 11.3) One thousand two hundred and threescore days is 1,260 or something that is coiled three and one half times. Three hundred sixty is one coil yet times three is 1080 and one half of 360 is 180. So 1080 plus 180 is 1,260. The two witnesses are the pin gala and Ida or the pineal and pituitary glands representing the masculine and feminine principles or electricity and magnetism respectively. Yet is looked at as a feminine energy, which is why the snake is shown in ancient cultures associated with women. For instance in ancient Tamare, the Khmenu a word meaning eight which the Greeks called Ogdoads are four frogs and four snakes. The snakes represent the female (F) and the frogs are male (M) as the sperm and tadpole are synonymous.

Khmenu (Ogdoads)

Eight is the number associated with Djehuti, Tehuti, later known as Thoth and Hermes Trismegistus at Hermopolis aka Memphis, which came from the word Men Nefer. He is the master of the number eight and is considered a lunar deity. The Egyptian denderah, the Arabic dome of the rock, Sumerian Inanna symbol and Buddhist dharma symbol all are based on the Eight and feminine principles.

Denderah

This is about life and is one of the reasons the Egyptian cross, the Ankh, is used as a symbol of life. The Khmenu are Amun (M), Amunet (F), Nun (M), Nunet (F), Kek (M) and Keket (F), Heh (M) and Hehet (F). If you take the first letter of each Khmenu you get the word ANKH which looks like the joining of the phallus and the reproductive organs of the woman.

GOD, THE BRAIN, THE BIBLE AND YOUR BODY

Ankh

Eight is the atomic number of oxygen. Ox is astrologically Taurus, which is a feminine symbol, and in astrology, the eighth symbol is Scorpio, which rules the generative region where the sacrum is located. The sacrum is also where the original eight cells in mitosis are stationed. In human adult dentition, there are eight teeth in each quadrant. The Eight tooth is called the wisdom tooth and wisdom is for the female deity, Sophia.

Alchemically, the sex act is shown with the fire and water alchemical signs. Fire represents red, is the triangle pointing up, and represents masculinity. Water is the blue triangle and points down signifying femininity. Fire being masculine moves in an up and outward direction like the phallus, whereas water is blue and feminine because it pulls down and in, as does the vagina or gravity. Aries a masculine astrology sign is fire aka the sun that is up in the head. Water is down aka Pisces a feminine astrology sign, which is located at the feet according to medical astrology.

Triangles

The dualism is also found all over the bible for example, the bible contains the story of two warring gods, the sun God and the moon God. The sun God is known biblicaly as El which is short for Elohim and the moon God is Ah or Yahweh also known as Ba'al. In addition, this sun god rules and resides in the head of hue mans. Whereas the moon god rules the lower nature where the stomach is located. Take for instance the word abdomen which can be viewed as Abd mean slave and Omen meaning

GOD, THE BRAIN, THE BIBLE AND YOUR BODY

slave of the oath. Abdomen is the ab meaning father and demon is from the latin word Daemon meaning spirit from Greek Daimon meaning deity lesser God. The abdomen has other words in english that replace it, one is belly a word meaning to swell or become angry. Another is the word stomach which is known as the second brain because it has the same material as the brain. The belly is Bel or Ba'al. In Hebrew you make a word possesive by adding a yod or I(y) to the end of it. Thus Bel made possessive is belly making Belly mean my God. Ba'al later became bowel or bow to El. Lastly, another name for abdomen is gut. Gut is a derivative of the German word Gott which is where the English word God gets its origin. So when we find Again, the devil taketh him up into an exceeding high mountain, and sheweth him all the kingdoms of the world, and the glory of them; 9 And saith unto him, All these things will I give thee, if thou wilt fall down and worship me. (Matt. 4.8-9) This is symbolically speaking of the lower nature (ba'al, belly, devil) trying to deceived humans to stop worshipping God or the higher nature (El, temple). As stated previously, the stomach is known as the second brain and now science has begun to study the stomach for cures to ailments in the brain. Recently an article suggested that Parkinson's disease may begin in the stomach.

GOD, THE BRAIN, THE BIBLE AND YOUR BODY

Parkinson's disease may start in the gut, groundbreaking new research suggests. Scientists have found the first ever-conclusive link between gut microbes and the development of Parkinson's-like movement disorders in mice. They managed to alleviate the symptoms using antibiotic treatment. The discovery, published today in the journal Cell, could overhaul medical research and treatment of Parkinson's. It suggests that probiotic or prebiotic therapies have the potential to alleviate the symptoms of the second most common neurodegenerative disease in the United States. 'This research reveals that a neurodegenerative disease may have its origins in the gut, and not only in the brain as had been previously thought,' says senior study author Sarkis Mazmanian of the California Institute of Technology. 'The discovery that changes in the microbiome may be involved in Parkinson's disease is a paradigm shift and opens entirely new possibilities for treating patients.' Parkinson's disease affects an estimated one million people and 1 percent of the United States population over 60 years of age. The disease is caused by the accumulation of abnormally shaped α-synuclein proteins in neurons, leading to particularly toxic effects in dopamine-releasing cells located in brain regions that control movement. As a result, patients experience debilitating symptoms such as tremors, muscle stiffness, slowness of movement, and impaired gait. Currently, therapies focus on increasing dopamine levels in the brain. However, these treatments can cause serious side effects and often lose effectiveness over time. To address the need for safer and more effective treatments, Mazmanian and first author Timothy

GOD, THE BRAIN, THE BIBLE AND YOUR BODY

Sampson of the California Institute of Technology turned to gut microbes as an intriguing possibility. Patients with Parkinson's disease have an altered gut microbiome, and gastrointestinal problems such as constipation often precede motor deficits by many years in these individuals Read more: http://www.dailymail.co.uk/health/article-3992234/Parkinson-s-start-GUT-not-brain-Study-finds-link-disease-gut-microbes.html#ixzz4RiBRc9Rv

Your body's 7 CHAKRAS

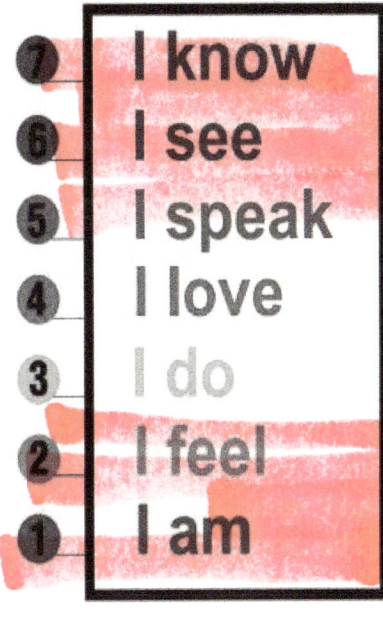

7. I know
6. I see
5. I speak
4. I love
3. I do
2. I feel
1. I am

Chakras

The word Chakra (चक्र) comes from the Sanskrit word for wheel or circle and has been described as a spinning wheel of light. Chakras are also energy seats in the body that generally correspond to the seven major organs of the endocrine system and glands in your body. There are a total of nine chakras that encompass the body. Each chakra emits a color that is based on the color scheme of the rainbow: violet, indigo, blue, green, yellow, orange and red. The other two colors are ultra violet above the crown chakra and infrared below the root chakra. However, because they vibrate at frequencies the human eye cannot recognize without the aid of machines, they are not generally recognized. The seven chakras have secret names starting from the bottom. Lam, Vam, Ram, Yam, Ham, Aum and all or Allah is the crown chakra. Each chakra corresponds to seven vowels: A (alpha), E' (epsilon), E" (eta), I (iota), O'(omicron), U(upsilon), O"(omega) – and make the sacred tone OM, AUM; AAAUUUUMMMM. The first of these chakras starting at the top of the head is the Crown chakra.

CROWN CHAKRA – PURPLE

The Crown chakra is located at the top (crown) of the head, the brain. It is represented by 1000 petals and is ruled by the planets Saturn and Uranus. The symbol for the crown is the lotus plant. The crown chakra motto is "I know I understand". It is known to vibrate on the Musical scale of "Tee" and corresponds to the musical note B. It is associated with the pineal/pituitary gland. Its chemical element is nitrogen. Foods good for the crown chakra are carrots. Carrots were originally purple prior to becoming hybrids.

BROW/3RD EYE CHAKRA – INDIGO

The brow or third eye chakra is located above the eyebrows around the center of the forehead. It is represented by 96 petals and is ruled astrologically by the planets Cancer and Leo. The motto for the brow chakra is "I see". It is known to vibrate on the musical scale of la "lah" and corresponds to the musical note A. It is also associated with the pineal and pituitary glands as well. Its chemical element is iron. Foods good for the brow chakra are bilberries a cousin of the blueberry.

THROAT CHAKRA – BLUE

Next is the throat chakra which is located in the Adam's apple region of the neck. It corresponds to the thyroid gland in the neck. It is represented by 16 petals and is ruled by the planets Jupiter and Mercury. The element ether is associated with this chakra. The motto for the throat chakra is "I speak". The musical note of G corresponds to this chakra and the musical scale associated with the throat chakra is So "soh". Copper and Tin are the metals associated with the throat chakra. Foods known to enrich the throat chakra are fruits that grow on trees: apples, apricots, peaches, pears and plums

HEART CHAKRA - GREEN

The center of the chest and heart is the location for the fourth and balancing chakra called the Heart Chakra. It is associated with the thymus gland and heart/lungs. Because of its association with the lungs, it has been assigned Air as its element. A total of 12 petals represent the heart chakra which has a motto of "I Love". It vibrates to the musical note F and the scale of Fa "fah". Gold is the metal associated with the Heart Chakra. (Child is born with a heart of gold – way of the world EWF). Mercury and Venus are the planets associated with the heart chakra (Venus goddess of love). Green leafy foods are good for the heart chakra. kale, kelp, lettuces, spinach and sprouts as well as green teas.

GOD, THE BRAIN, THE BIBLE AND YOUR BODY

NAVEL SOLAR CHAKRA - YELLOW
Found in the center of the stomach roughly two inches under center of rib cage and diaphragm is where the navel chakra is positioned. The digestive system is assigned to the navel chakra. 10 petals are associated with this chakra. The statement I Will" is the motto for the Navel chakra. The musical scale Me and musical note E is the vibratory frequency associated with the navel chart. Ruled by the planets Mars and the Sun its metal association is Tin. Mars being the god of war and weaponry is related to the fire element as is the navel chakra. Whole grain breads and cereals, granola, flax and rice are some good foods for this chakra.

SACRAL CHAKRA - ORANGE
The Sacral chakra is located 2 inches below the belly button and also around the lower back region of the body where the sexual organs are located. Thus the ovaries and testes are associated with the sacral charka. It is associated with 6 lotus petals and the metal Iron. It has a motto that states "I feel". D is the musical note associated with the sacral/sacrum chakra as well as the musical scale of Re (Ray). It is ruled by the Moon. The moon has an effect on all water, thus, the sacral charka is related to the fourth element, water. Since this chakra is associated with reproduction, fruits with seeds are particularly helpful particularly mangos, melons, oranges and strawberries.

ROOT CHAKRA - RED

The last of the chakras is the root chakra which is found at the base of the tailbone, spine or coccyx; the perineum (between the anus and genitals regions of the body). It is also associated with the adrenals in the body. It is represented by a four petal lotus and is ruled by the Sun and planet Saturn. Its metal correspondence is Lead. The musical vibration for the Root chakra is the musical note of C and the scale of Do "doh". It uses the motto "I am". The root chakra represents the element Earth. Root foods and radishes are good for to energize the root chakra.

The author wants the reader to recognize how each chakra has a color and the foods associated with that color are the same as the chakra color vibration. Therefore, it advised to base your diet on this model. As even the bible teaches And God said, Let the earth bring forth grass, the herb yielding seed, and the fruit tree yielding fruit after his kind, whose seed is in itself, upon the earth: and it was so. 12 And the earth brought forth grass, and herb yielding seed after his kind, and the tree yielding fruit, whose seed was in itself, after his kind: and God saw that it was good. (Gen. 1.11-12) God later states that this is meat for you. "And God said, Behold, I have given you every herb bearing seed, which is upon the face of all the earth, and every tree, in the which is the fruit of a tree yielding seed; to you it shall be for meat. 30 And to every beast of the earth, and to every fowl of the air, and to everything that creepeth upon the earth, wherein there is life, I have given every green herb for meat: and it was so. (Gen. 1.29-30) As you read, you recognize that God has also designated the same diet for everything on the planet inclusive of beasts and birds, not that beasts and birds should be food for you. The Father of western medicine Hippocrates said ""Let food be thy medicine and medicine be thy food."

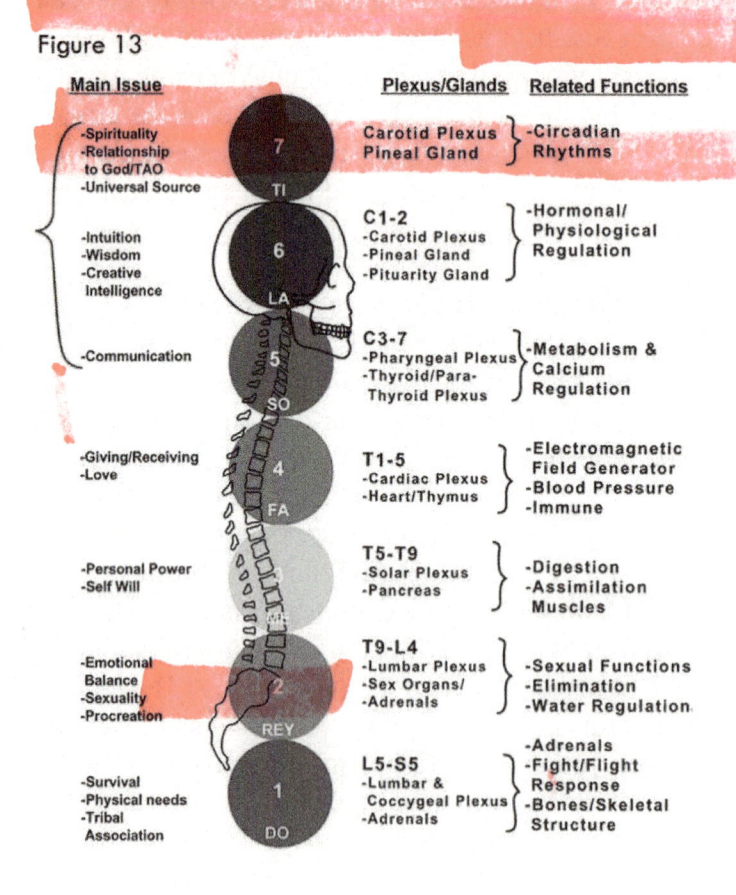

Figure 13

Main Issue	Plexus/Glands	Related Functions
-Spirituality -Relationship to God/TAO -Universal Source	Carotid Plexus Pineal Gland	-Circadian Rhythms
-Intuition -Wisdom -Creative Intelligence	C1-2 -Carotid Plexus -Pineal Gland -Pituarity Gland	-Hormonal/ Physiological Regulation
-Communication	C3-7 -Pharyngeal Plexus -Thyroid/Para-Thyroid Plexus	-Metabolism & Calcium Regulation
-Giving/Receiving -Love	T1-5 -Cardiac Plexus -Heart/Thymus	-Electromagnetic Field Generator -Blood Pressure -Immune
-Personal Power -Self Will	T5-T9 -Solar Plexus -Pancreas	-Digestion -Assimilation Muscles
-Emotional Balance -Sexuality -Procreation	T9-L4 -Lumbar Plexus -Sex Organs/ -Adrenals	-Sexual Functions -Elimination -Water Regulation
-Survival -Physical needs -Tribal Association	L5-S5 -Lumbar & Coccygeal Plexus -Adrenals	-Adrenals -Fight/Flight Response -Bones/Skeletal Structure

Adrenal Glands

GOD, THE BRAIN, THE BIBLE AND YOUR BODY

As you see the eight octave scale is represented in the body as each chakra gives off a musical vibration/frequency and tone. Put simply an octave is a musical interval of eight notes. Musical pitch is defined by frequency and usually expressed in Hertz (Hz).

Color	Wavelength interval	Frequency interval
Red	~ 700–635 nm	~ 430–480 THz
Orange	~ 635–590 nm	~ 480–510 THz
Yellow	~ 590–560 nm	~ 510–540 THz
Green	~ 560–520 nm	~ 540–580 THz
Cyan	~ 520–490 nm	~ 580–610 THz
Blue	~ 490–450 nm	~ 610–670 THz
Violet	~ 450–400 nm	~ 670–750 THz

Wavelengths

which measures vibrations per second. Our body has a musical pitch of 432 Hz which coincides with the frequency of nature. Interestingly enough the number 432 is a multiple of the speed of light which is 186,624 miles per second. (432*432 = 186,624 or 299,792,458 meters per second) There are various forms of light which are infrared, ultraviolet which as previously stated are invisible to humans, whereas "regular" light is visible to the human eye. The speed of the vibration determines if that light is visible to humans. The energy behind the sun although black gives off white light. White light is comprised of all the colors of the visible color spectrum. The light hits particles or rain drops in the atmospere and gives us the seven sphered spectrum such as the colors of a rainbow. The rain drops act as a prism which dispenses the different variations in colors. The highest frequency produces the color violet where as the lowest frequency produces the red color. As the frequency hits the prism at various angles the various colors of the electromagnetic sprectrum are produced.

A slower form of light is sound waves, which are a lot slower than light waves. Sound waves move at a rate of 1,125 feet per second or about 340 meters per second. Sound waves travel through any type of substance, whether solid, liquid or gas, whereas light travels through empty space. When sound is put in a special vacuum it can move faster than light. When light or sound waves encounter a substance they cause that substance to vibrate. These vibrations can be both high and low frequency. Low frequency sound waves produce low tones while high frequency waves create high-pitched tones. One of the most important facts to understand about both light and sound is that both are forms of energy that move in waves. Thus these chakras are light that also give off sound. Mercier states "As humans, we exist within the 49th Octave of Vibration of the electromagnetic light spectrum. Below this range are barely visible radiant heat, then invisible infrared, television and radiowaves, sound and brain waves; above it is barely visible ultraviolet, then the invisible frequencies of chemicals and perfumes, followed by x-rays, gamma rays, radium rays and unknown cosmic rays" Mercier, Patricia (2007). The Chakra Bible: the definitive guide to working with chakras. London: Godsfield Press/Octopus Publishing. p. 12. ISBN 978-1-84181-320-2.

22/7 is in fact an expression of three consecutive octaves of resonance. An octave, as everyone knows, comprises seven fundamental notes: Do-re-mi-fa-sol-la-ti. The eighth note, Do, a repeat of the first but with double the pitch frequency, is the first note of the second octave. Accordingly the eighth note of the second octave – again, Do – is the first note of the third. Taken together these three octaves contain twenty-two notes.

GOD, THE BRAIN, THE BIBLE AND YOUR BODY

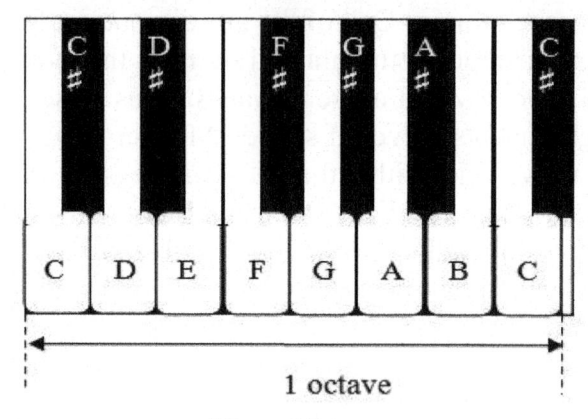

Piano Notes

This configuration expresses in exact scientific terms everything you need to know to understand the General Theory of just about everything. All one need do to appreciate this is to remember the key musical numbers incorporated within it. These are: 3, 4, 7, 8, 22, and 64. Three, the number of the Trinity, is the number of octaves encoded in pi. Four is the number of base-notes (Dos) in three consecutive octaves. Seven is the number of intervals between the notes of the major scale. Eight is the number of individual notes in the major scale. Twenty-two is the number of notes in three consecutive scales or octaves. And, according to the law of three forces, the three octaves incorporated in pi are each sub-divisible into three octaves apiece, giving an inner formula of nine octaves, or sixty-four notes. So eight is the constant, and sixty-four, is the square of it. In the Koran, there is a crucial chapter on the sacred light of Allah – chapter sixty-four.
http://www.academia.edu/1618652/Egyptian_fractions_and_the_ancient_science_of_harmonics

GOD, THE BRAIN, THE BIBLE AND YOUR BODY

This is also encoded in the Holy Bible as The Ray of Creation, which starts on Day 0 with the intention of the Lord God (Almighty) to create the whole of reality, mostly called 'the world'. This is the tone of *Do* from *Dominus*, a Latin word meaning the Lord. On Day 1, God separated the light from the darkness. This is the separation of the light (*yang*) of all the stars (or *Sidera* in Latin) from the darkness (*yin*) of the rest of the universe (or macrocosm). This is the tone of *Si* from Sidera (or all galaxies). On Day 2, God said, "Let there be a firmament in the midst of the waters, and let it separate the waters from the waters." The 'waters' is a reference to a galaxy. The galaxy we can see in the midst of the firmament is our own galaxy called the Milky Way. This is the tone of *La* from *Lactea*, meaning milk. On Day 3, God said, "Let the waters under the heaven temples be gathered together into one place." In this level of Creation, 'water' refers to light. The gathering of light into one place is a reference to our sun Helios. This is the tone of *Sol*, meaning the sun. On Day 4, God said, "Let there be lights in the firmament of the heavens to separate the day from the night; and let them be for signs and for seasons and for days and years." These lights in the firmament that enable us to keep track of time are the visible planets of our solar system. These planets play a key role in astrology, which provides us a scientific description of fate. This is the tone of *Fa* from *Fata*, meaning fate. On Day 5, God said, "Let the waters bring forth swarms of living creatures, and let birds fly above the earth across the firmament of the heavens." Again, the 'waters' that bring forth living creatures refer to light, meaning all cosmic energies that support biological life. The microcosm includes all living creatures on our mother planet called Terra (Gaia means Mother Terra). Next, the 'birds' that fly above the microcosm of Terra across the firmament of the heavens refer to the stars of the macrocosm. This is the tone of *Mi* as the abbreviation of the Latin word *Microcosmus*. On Day 6, God said, "Let us make man in our image, after our likeness; and let them reign over the fish of the sea, and over the birds of the air, and over the cattle, and over the entire planet, and over every creeping thing that creeps upon the planet." This is the tone of *Re* of Regina, meaning Regent. Humanity's role is to reign or rule over biological live on Terra. At this level of the Ray of Creation, the moon Luna reigns (as a Regent) over the waters of Terra. On Day 7 we find again the tone of *Do* from Dominus, meaning Lord. Or to put this differently, the seventh Day is the Day of the Lord.

Tone	Latin	English	Meaning Day	Verse
Do	*Dominus*	Lord	The Lord 0	Genesis 2:4
Si	*Sidera*	Stars	all galaxies 1	Genesis 1:16
La	*Lactea*	Milk	our Milky Way 2	
Sol	*Sol*	Sun	our sun Helios 3	Genesis 19:23
Fa	*Fata*	Fate	our solar system 4	
Mi	*Microcosmus*	Microcosm	our planet Terra 5	Genesis 1:1
Re	*Regina*	Regent	our moon Luna 6	Genesis 37:9
Do	*Dominus*	Lord	The Lord 7	Genesis 2:4

GOD, THE BRAIN, THE BIBLE AND YOUR BODY

Misinterpreted symbols

Baphomet

You have been taught that the symbol on the right of the baphomet is evil. That is the trick the lower natured ones have used to keep you from investigating the real and/or original meaning behind these ancient symbols. The real science behind this symbol is again found in the esoteric body. The bible begins with Genesis and ends in Revelations. All thoughts are formulated and revealed in the head where the cerebrum and cerebellum are located. The image also shows the femur bone of the thigh. This is code for the phallus and if a man was to make an oath or testify he had to put his hand under

GOD, THE BRAIN, THE BIBLE AND YOUR BODY

another mans "thigh". The word thigh in Hebrew is Yakul and means to swell or soft which refers to the phallus of men. And Abraham said unto his eldest servant of his house, that ruled over all that he had, Put, I pray thee, thy hand under my thigh: (Gen. 24.2) Testifying comes from the word Teste and Testa meaning scrotum or the generative region of a man. According to Etymonline.com Testa also means skull C14: from Medieval Latin *testerium,* from Late Latin *testa* a skull, from Latin: shell. So when one looks at this image from its original esoteric meaning, it's telling you about the seven (7) chakras and how the revelations travel from the skull and down into the sacrum where the phallus is located. Further confirmation can be found by the Yale fraternity Skull and Bones who use as it's emblem an owl and the numbers 322 (3+2+2=7).   The owl is a symbol of wisdom and all knowledge is found in the skull.

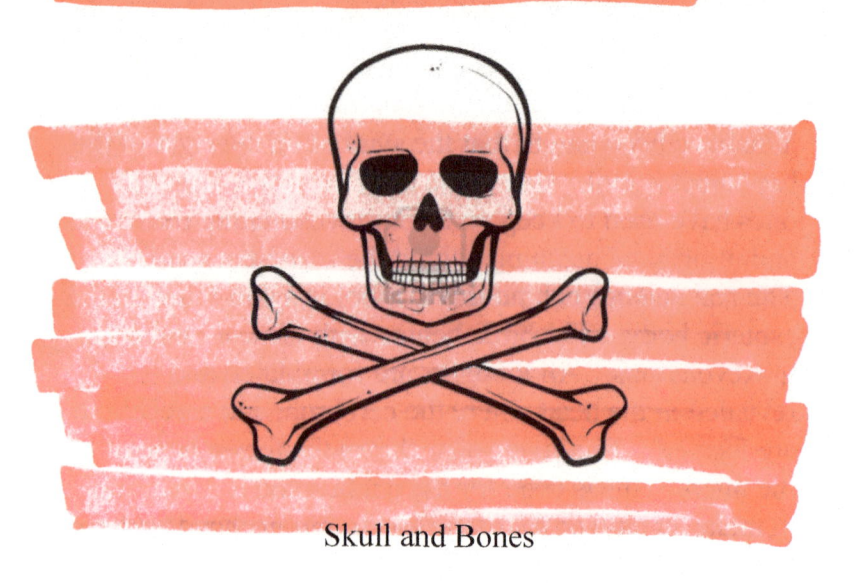

Skull and Bones

GOD, THE BRAIN, THE BIBLE AND YOUR BODY

According to the book Dictionary of Symbols, "Owls represent silent or higher wisdom, prophecy, mystery, healing power, hidden secrets, seeing in the darkness, spiritual sight, death, smelting, thunderbolt, purification, communion and a symbol of spirit or ghost leading from death to life. The hooting of the great horned owl is thought to be a harbinger of spring."

Another commonly misinterpreted figure is the Queen of Sheba. According to legend Sheba was actually a woman who sought out the great wisdom of the Israeli King, Solomon. The name Sheba is initially found in the book of Genesis and the sons of Cush; Seba, and Havilah, and Sabtah, and Raamah, and Sabtecha: and the sons of Raamah; Sheba, and Dedan. (Gen. 10.7) As you see from this verse, Sheba is/was a masculine name not a feminine name. The word Sheba is related to the Semitic word for Seven, Sheba/Shevah. It is also found in the word Beersheba a place Abraham visited. Sheba is part of the name of King Solomon's Hittite mother who was called Bath-sheba, which they translate as daughter of the oath "And David sent and inquired after the woman. And one said, Is not this Bath-sheba, the daughter of Eliam, the wife of Uriah the Hittite? (2 Sam. 11.3)

GOD, THE BRAIN, THE BIBLE AND YOUR BODY

Solomon

GOD, THE BRAIN, THE BIBLE AND YOUR BODY

According to the Ethiopian legend in their holy book the Kebra Negast, Sheba's other name was Makeda and she had a child with Solomon who is named Menelik I and this is one of the ways the Ethiopian claim ancestry into the Israelite nation. And when the queen of Sheba heard of the fame of Solomon concerning the name of the LORD, she came to prove him with hard questions. 2 And she came to Jerusalem with a very great train, with camels that bare spices, and very much gold, and precious stones: and when she was come to Solomon, she communed with him of all that was in her heart. 3 And Solomon told her all her questions: there was not anything hid from the king, which he told her not. 4 And when the queen of Sheba had seen all Solomon's wisdom, and the house that he had built, (1 Kings 10.1) Unfortunately, none of this is based on factual historical information regardless of much each group claims Makeda aka Sheba existed. If the Queen of Sheba did not exist then so too did Solomon not exist. Solomon is a play on the name of three solar deities, Sol from where the word Solar comes, Om and On an Egyptian solar deity. According to Manly P. Hall's Secret Teachings of All Ages it states "One expression of the solar energy is Solomon, whose name SOL-OM-ON is the name for the Supreme Light in three different languages. Yet the word Solomon can also be viewed as Soul of Man as the soul of man resides in the temple. If Solomon did not exist; neither did the famed Solomon's temple. The description of temple is found in the bible as well And the house, when it was in building, was built of stone made ready before it was brought thither: so that there was neither hammer nor axe nor any tool of iron heard in

GOD, THE BRAIN, THE BIBLE AND YOUR BODY

the house, while it was in building. 8 The door for the middle chamber was in the right side of the house: and they went up with winding stairs into the middle chamber and out of the middle into the third. (1 Kings 6.7-8) This is referencing the human body. The only temple built without the use of hands is the human temple. Verse eight speaks of the winding staircase and that is the spinal column and ends on the right side, which is right side of the brain the same place Jesus resides in heaven. When the bible speaks of the Queen of the south coming to visit Solomon, it is speaking of traveling from the root chakra found in the southern part of the body and rising up to the head or Solomon's temple where God dwells and where the wisdom is stored. The temple is also built using a unit of measurements called a cubit. A cubit is 18 inches which happens to be the same length of the spinal column of the average man. This is the reason the mythical number 666 is used as well, as three 6's is 18. Now the weight of gold that came to Solomon in one year was six hundred threescore and six talents of gold. (1 Kings 10.14) This number equals 666 for 600 plus threescore – a score is 20 – so three score is 3 times 20 or 60 and finally the number 6. The Queen of Sheba brought Solomon gold symbolically and this is an alchemical process used by ancient alchemists to turn lead into gold. Sheba by getting the wisdom from Solomon that she sought gained the wisdom. She was no longer being lead; she attained wisdom and therefore became goaled. You too must be able to turn the lead to gold and go from being led by others to having your own goals. Sheba represents the seven chakras found in the body.

GOD, THE BRAIN, THE BIBLE AND YOUR BODY

THE SNAKE HANDLERS

Snake Handler

GOD, THE BRAIN, THE BIBLE AND YOUR BODY

A few years ago, the astrological and zodiacal world was in an uproar of the supposed finding of a new constellation called Ophiuchus. What was not known to the novice astrologist is that Ophiuchus was one of the original 48 constellations identified by Ptolemy and originally identified by the Africans as Imhotep. Ophiuchus was touted as the 13th zodiac sign and would cover the period from November 29 to December 17 on the Gregorian calendar. In Islam, this constellation was known as *Al-Ḥawwa'* "the snake-charmer". So in keeping with the theme of this work, the author will make the connection with this constellation and the human body. Readers of the bible should know the mother of all living known as Eve in English is called Hawwah in Hebrew as well as in the Arabic of the Quran. A snake charmer is also someone who talks to snakes and this is what Hawwah aka Eve did in the infamous story found in Genesis 3. For her part in this, the God of the bible And I will put enmity between thee and the woman, and between thy seed and her seed; it shall bruise thy head, and thou shalt bruise his heel. (Gen. 3.15) This is symbolism for the Ophiuchus constellation, which shows a man standing with a snake around his sacrum yet standing on the head of a scorpion. Therefore you get the story where the woman's seed or descendant shall put his foot on the serpent (the Scorpio) which will bruise the scorpions head but the scorpion will bruise the man's foot. Virgo is always head up and Scorpio is at her feet. The body of the serpent with the red star Antares, she is bruising him on the head and him on her heel.

GOD, THE BRAIN, THE BIBLE AND YOUR BODY

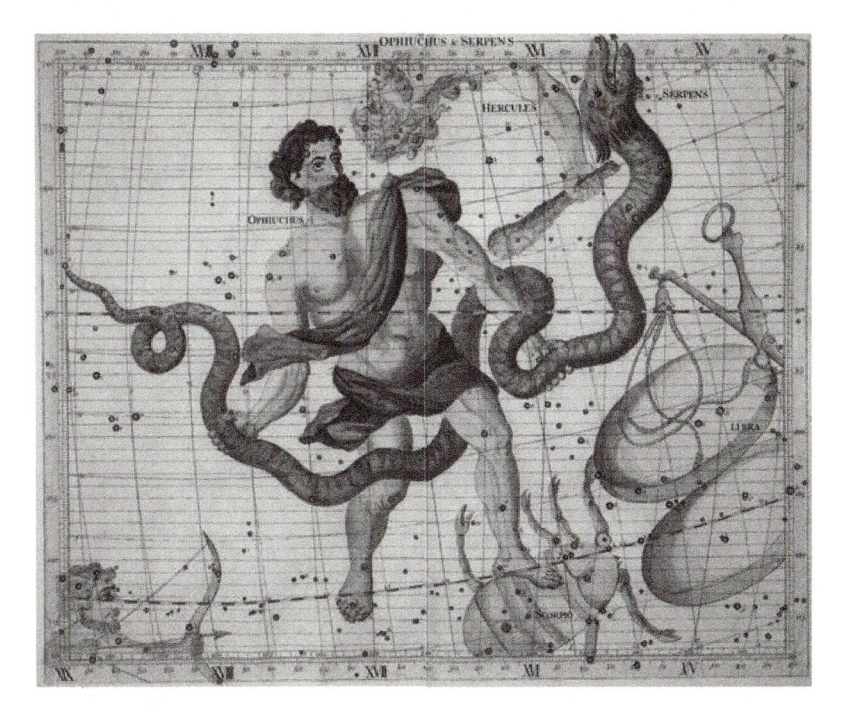

Ophiuchus

The snake symbolizes the kunalini, which is called the coiled serpent. The Kundalini is a feminine energy that is coiled three and one half times at the base of the spine where the sacrum is located. Once the kunalini is awaken via meditation and various self-discipline activities it activates the seven chakras and unfurls reaching to the skull. This is shown on the Namuz of ancient Egyptian pharaohs as coming out of the forehead or third eye region of the skull.

GOD, THE BRAIN, THE BIBLE AND YOUR BODY

Ra and Apep

This ancient African science accounts for the story in the bible when the Hebrew Moses turned his rod into a snake and the Africans did the same "trick". Now Moses kept the flock of Jethro his father in law, the priest of Midian: and he led the flock to the backside of the desert, and came to the mountain of God, even to Horeb. 2 And the angel of the LORD appeared unto him in a flame of fire out of the midst of a bush: and he looked, and, behold, the bush burned with fire, and the bush was not consumed. (Exod. 3.1-2) Moses went up the back side which is the backside of the body and is also where the kundalini is located. The mountain of God is the head. The wilderness is the act of going into

GOD, THE BRAIN, THE BIBLE AND YOUR BODY

mediation and lastly the burning bush is the spinal column and the nervous system which has branches like a tree but is not consumed by the fire known as the solar plexus where the fourth chakra the heart chakra is located. Further we read And Moses answered and said, But, behold, they will not believe me, nor hearken unto my voice: for they will say, The LORD hath not appeared unto thee. 2 And the LORD said unto him, What is that in thine hand? And he said, A rod. 3 And he said, Cast it on the ground. And he cast it on the ground, and it became a serpent; and Moses fled from before it. 4 And the LORD said unto Moses, Put forth thine hand, and take it by the tail. And he put forth his hand, and caught it, and it became a rod in his hand: (Exod. 4.1-4) This again is not to be taken literally but is symbolism as the rod is the spine. Moses took the snake by the tail because the spine begins with the coccyx, the tail bone, which are four fused bones. This is showing when you relinquish control of trying to control the serpent energy the kundalini raises however, when you take the snake in your hand, you are in control and it turns back into a rod and you lose your power. The author hopes the reader recognizes that Moses is also a snake charmer being he as well as the Africans handled the snake. The medical industry adopted this knowledge from Imhotep one of the first recognized doctors. This is why the medical industry uses the caduceus as it is obviously the spine with the kundalini and the wings are a section in your head called the sphenoid bone. The sphenoid bone protects the pituitary gland which rules the endocrine system. The endocrine glands are where the seven chakras are situated in the body.

GOD, THE BRAIN, THE BIBLE AND YOUR BODY

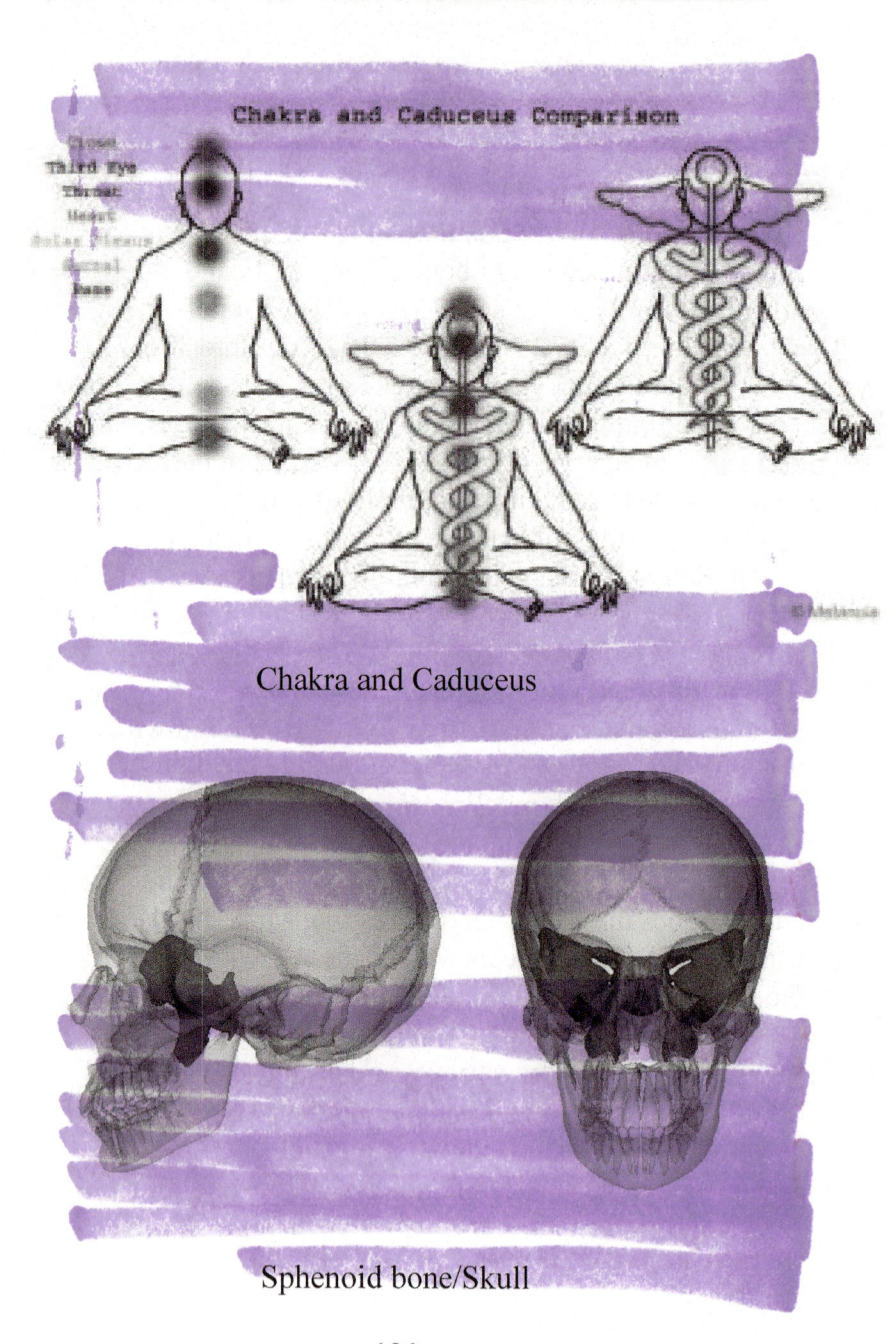

Chakra and Caduceus

Sphenoid bone/Skull

GOD, THE BRAIN, THE BIBLE AND YOUR BODY

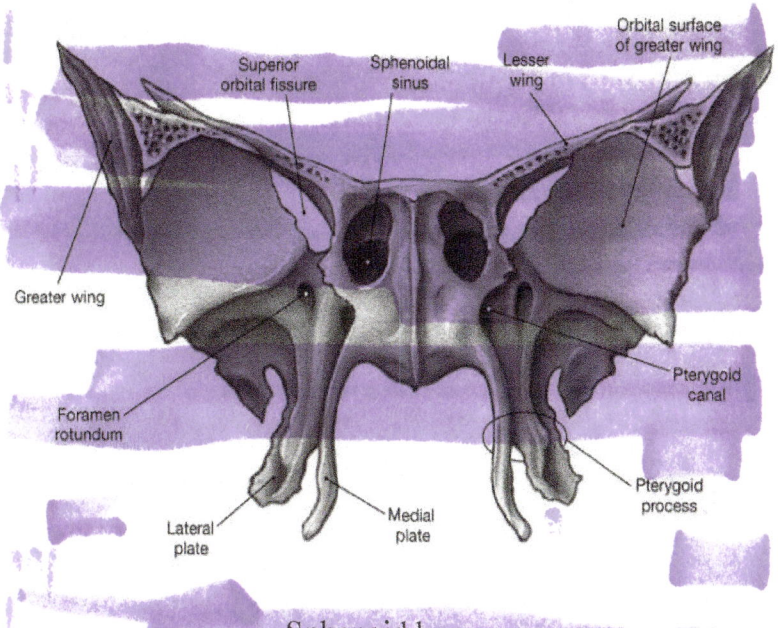

Sphenoid bone

The pituitary gland is a pea-sized gland located in the center of the skull, inferior to the hypothalamus of the brain and posterior to the bridge of the nose. It is an important link between the nervous and endocrine systems and releases many hormones which affect growth, sexual development, metabolism and human reproduction. The pituitary gland is termed the "Master Gland" because it directs other organs and endocrine glands, such as the adrenal glands, to suppress or induce hormone production.
http://www.innerbody.com/image/endo01.html

GOD, THE BRAIN, THE BIBLE AND YOUR BODY

The pituitary gland, also known as the hypophysis, is connected to the hypothalamus of the brain by a tiny isthmus of nervous tissue called the infundibulum It sits within a small cavity in the sphenoid bone of the skull known as the hypophyseal fossa. Thus the sphenoid bone surrounds and protects the delicate pituitary gland from damage by external forces.

Therefore, the sun with healings in his wings is the pituitary gland that is protected by the sphenoid bone or wings. But unto you that fear my name shall the Sun of righteousness arise with healing in his wings; and ye shall go forth, and grow up as calves of the stall. (Mal 4.2) One of the functions of the pituitary is to secrete a neurotransmitter that gives pain relief. Additionally, the portion of the brain where this is located is in the cerebrum which is ruled by Taurus hence the reference to calves of the stall. In what's termed medical astrology or iatromathematics each of the twelve zodiacs rules a portion of your body.

GOD, THE BRAIN, THE BIBLE AND YOUR BODY

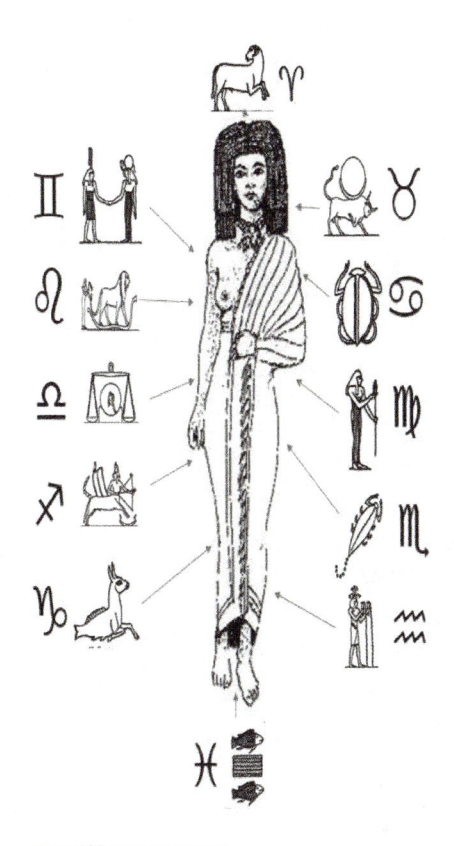

Iatromathematics/Medical Astrology

GOD, THE BRAIN, THE BIBLE AND YOUR BODY

Tribe of Israel	Zodiac	Body Part
Reuben	Aquarius	Shins
Simon	Gemini	Right Arm
Levi	Gemini	Left Arm
Judah	Leo	Heart
Issachar	Taurus	Lower jaw/neck
Zebulun	Pisces	Feet
Dan	Scorpio	Reproductive Organs
Naphtali	Capricorn	Knees
Gad	Aries	Head
Asher	Libra	Kidneys
Joseph	Sagittarius	Hips
Benjamin	Cancer	Chest
Dinah	Virgo	Stomach

The Africans also used this representation of the spinal column to correlate it to the whole of the Nile valley via the Hapi better known as the Nile River. Notice in Busiris the same area of the head where there pyramids are located as found in the chapter "the brain and the bible". According to the Leyden (Leiden) Papyrus found in Thebes in the 3rd Century A.D. – "All the gods are three, Amun Ra and Ptah who have no equals". Ra is the head, Ptah is the Body. Thebes, Heliopolis and Memphis. When a message comes from Heaven is it heard in Heliopolis, repeated in Memphis to Ptah. As you view the image below, you will notice Memphis is located where the throat chakra resides and this is why in the Leyden papyrus it is repeated to Ptah the body.

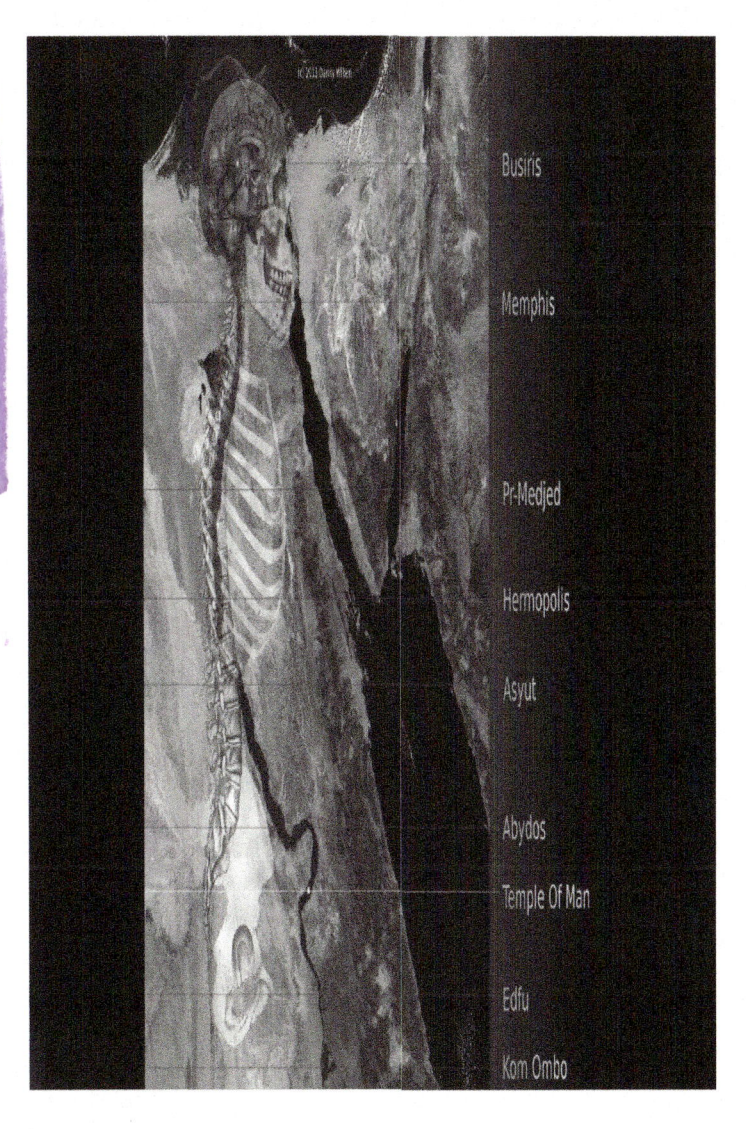

Nile River

GOD, THE BRAIN, THE BIBLE AND YOUR BODY

The Africans were so into cosmology and cosmogony that almost everything they depicted was representing of the axiom 'as above so below'. You also find in their hieroglyphs the zjed pillar which at times represented the spinal column. It was the foundation of the temple, just as the spinal column or cubit was the base of King Solomon's temple. Coincidently Nathan the prophet called Solomon Jedidiah. And David comforted Bathsheba his wife, and went in unto her, and lay with her: and she bare a son, and he called his name Solomon: and the LORD loved him. 25 And he sent by the hand of Nathan the prophet; and he called his name Jedidiah, because of the LORD. (2nd Sam. 12.24) A cubit is 18 inches and is the same amount of inches in the male spinal column.

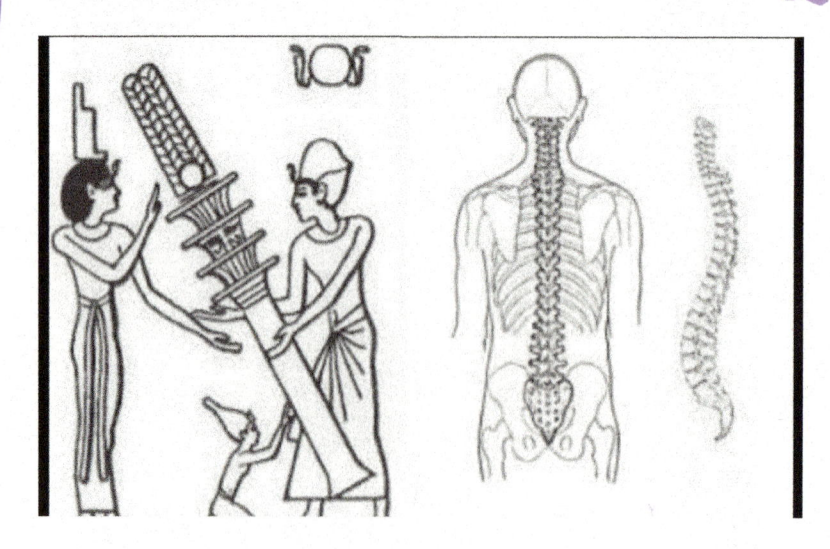

Zjed/Spinal column

GOD, THE BRAIN, THE BIBLE AND YOUR BODY

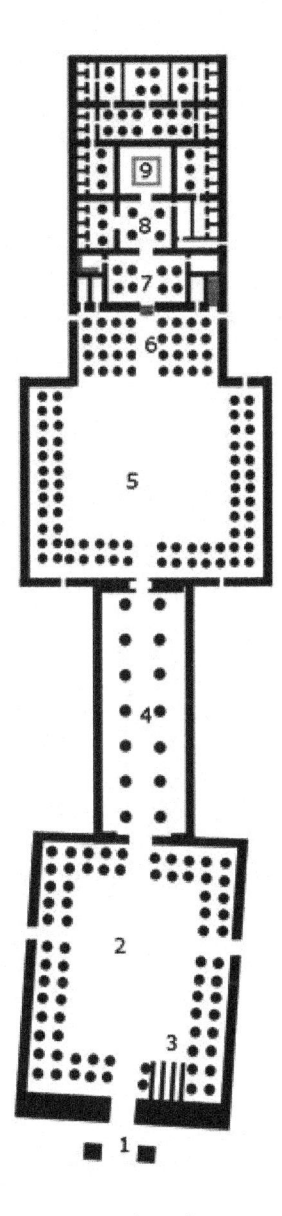

Temple of Man

GOD, THE BRAIN, THE BIBLE AND YOUR BODY

The ancient Africans initiated the idea of correlating their temples to the human body and creating structures that showed that correlation. The largest temple in the world located in Africa in what was once called Luxor meaning light in the Greek language, but is more commonly known as the Temple of man shows that correlation. As this knowledge spread over the African continent; the Dogon tribe of West Africa set up their villages with this same correspondence. As African cosmology spread across the globe, culture bandits established their religious temples to show this correspondence. In the bible in the book of Corinthians 3:16 it says you are the temple of god. The following images show temples built like human bodies.

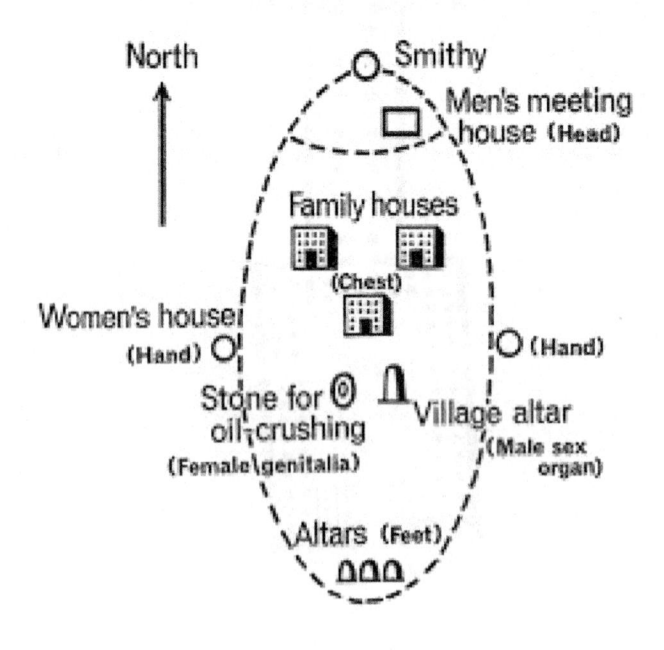

Dogon Village

GOD, THE BRAIN, THE BIBLE AND YOUR BODY

The Dogon built their village like the orbit of Sirius yet also incorporated the anatomy of the human body.

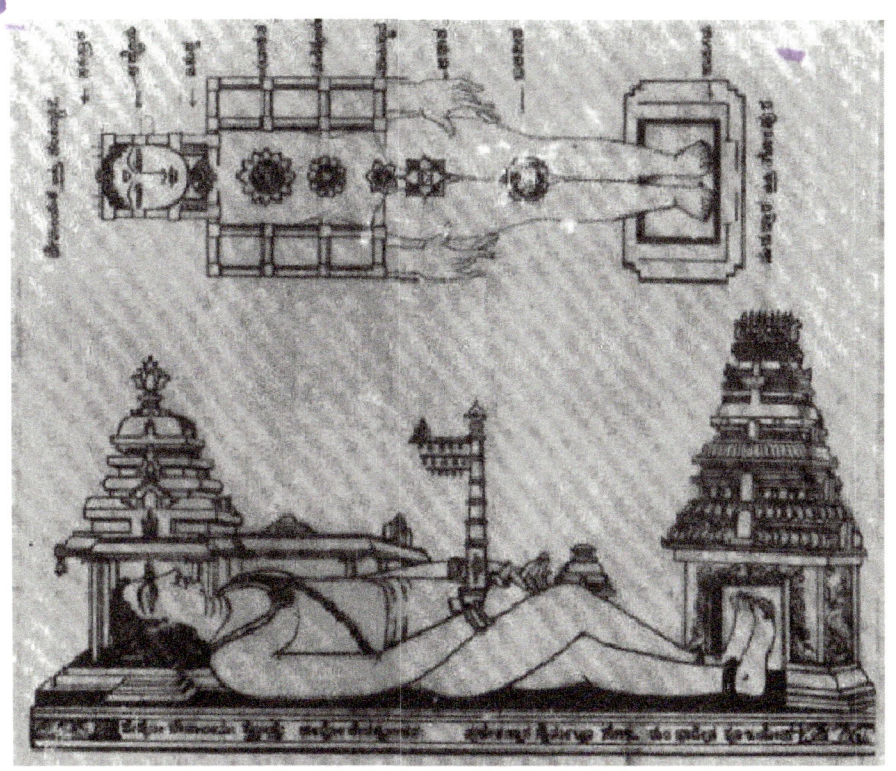

Stella Kramrish – the Hindu Temple

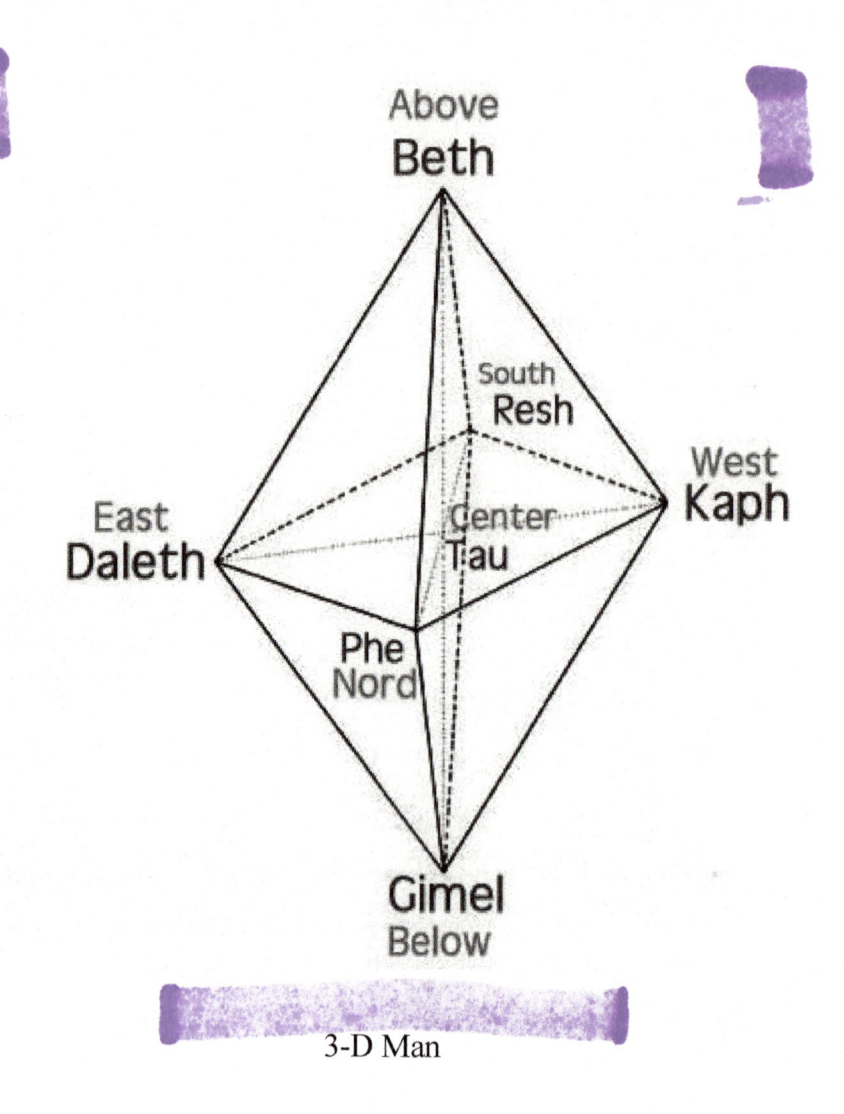

GOD, THE BRAIN, THE BIBLE AND YOUR BODY

Above
Beth

South
Resh

West
Kaph

East
Daleth

Center
Tau

Phe
Nord

Gimel
Below

3-D Man

GOD, THE BRAIN, THE BIBLE AND YOUR BODY

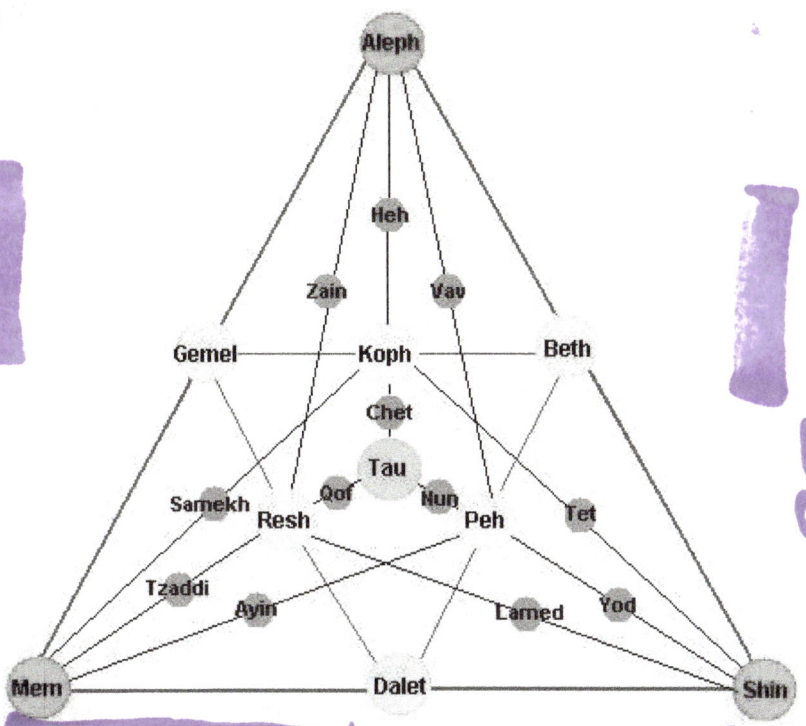

The Zohar (Kaballah) teaches the Jewish deity YHWH created man from the 22 Hebrew alphabet, specifically the three mother letters, Alif, Miim and Shin, the seven double letters aka the chakras and the 12 single letters or the 12 cranial nerves which created a three dimensional being. This three dimensional being is part alif (air), miim (water) and shin (fire) to become a solid; which is earth or carbon from the 22 amino acids. Thus, they wear the teffilin on their foreheads right around the third eye. Physiologically, the human skull has 22 bones. And the key of the house of David will I lay upon his shoulder; so he shall open, and none shall shut; and he shall shut, and none shall open. (Isa. 22.22)

GOD, THE BRAIN, THE BIBLE AND YOUR BODY

Later the Muhammadans who happened to live in an area long ago vacated by the Africans adopted this cube from the tefflin. The Ka'aba is an African symbol, as it has the same dimensions as the pyramids and serves the same purpose. One of the most important religious figures from Islam is Muhammad who is said to have wrote a special white horse with the face of a woman from Mecca where the Ka'aba is located to Jerusalem where Jews wear the tefflin. This distance coincidently is allegedly 666 nautical miles.

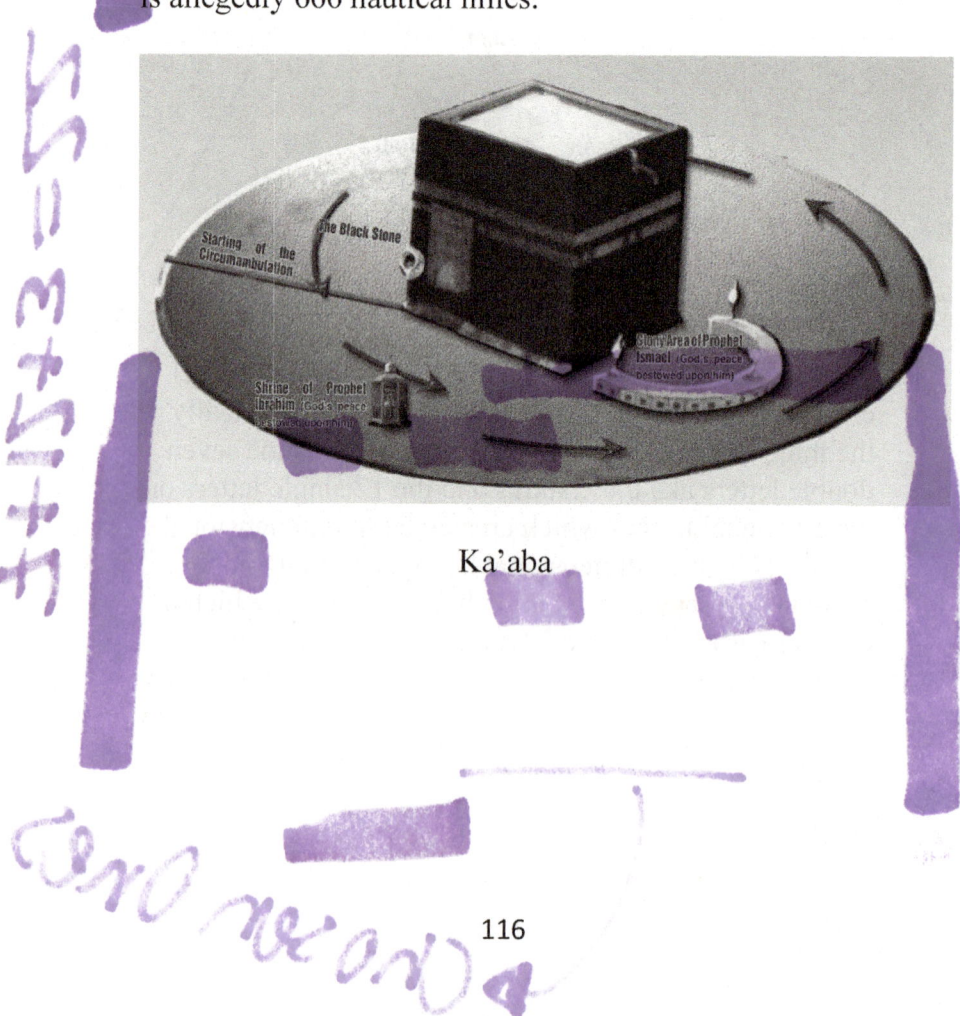

Ka'aba

GOD, THE BRAIN, THE BIBLE AND YOUR BODY

Temple of Man and Vatican City

Vatican city St Peters Basilica

Vatican City is built on 108 acres of land and coincides with the temple of Wa-set. The leg portion of the temple of man has the left leg moving forward and an angle at the knee portion. If you go inside the temple of man the columns are also cut at the knees. The thigh has the femur bone located within and the femur bone provides the largest amount of red blood cells for sustenance. Inside the temple the halls show a feast of sustenance. In the stomach region of the temple announces the birth of a deity. From the image of Vatican City we see the eight-pointed star area as the same area for the nave/stomach area which is where the sacrum is located. Inside the sacrum is the original eight cells from creation. The navel divides the total height of the body in the proportion of phi to 1. This is also why churches have a nave or the area below the altar where the benches and pews sit inside the church. Astronomically there is a constellation called Ara which means Altar. When viewed from earth the alter points down towards the earth. It was later co-opted into the bible and religion to be fire that will be sent from heaven down to earth and scorch the earth. In ancient Greek mythology, Ara was identified as the altar where the gods first made offerings and formed an alliance before defeating the Titans. As we see this image it brings to mind the following verses from the bible specifically identifying the body as the holy temple.

1 Corinthian 6:19 What? know ye not that your body is the temple of the Holy Ghost which is in you, which ye have of God, and ye are not your own?

1 Peter 2:5 you also, as living stones, are being built up as a spiritual house for a holy priesthood, to offer up spiritual sacrifices acceptable to God through Jesus Christ.

Ephesians 2:19-22 So then you are no longer strangers and aliens, but you are fellow citizens with the saints, and are of God's household, having been built on the foundation of the apostles and prophets, Christ Jesus Himself being the corner stone, in whom the whole building, being fitted together, is growing into a holy

GOD, THE BRAIN, THE BIBLE AND YOUR BODY

temple in the Lord, in whom you also are being built together into a dwelling of God in the Spirit

Thus Churches are merely replicas of human bodies and were not designed as the place to meet god and worship god. For by going inside and meditating will one meet God face to face, as Jacob did And Jacob called the name of the place Peniel: for I have seen God face to face and my life is preserved. (Gen. 32.30) Peniel is a play on the word Pineal.

As well, Jacob's ladder is a play on the first seven vertebrae in the spinal column. The first seven cervical vertebrae have been equated with the seven (7) archangels and the rest of the spinal vertebrae with bringing messages to the physical body by the angels ascending and descending. Notice on the image the superior vertebrae or archangels account for the first seven vertebrae then the lesser angels or inferior vertebrae begin after the first seven. Those seven arch angels are Gabriel (Atlas), Michael (Axis or Al Qubt), Raphael, Uriel, Raguel, Remiel and Sariel. These also correspond to the seven days of the week with Gabriel being Sunday and Sariel for Saturday. To reiterate the first vertebrae is the atlas and it holds the head to the body and was symbolized by the ancient Greek deity of Atlas. His punishment from Zeus was bearing the weight of the heavens on his shoulders.

GOD, THE BRAIN, THE BIBLE AND YOUR BODY

Dens of axis
Groove for vertebral artery and first cervical nerve
SUPERIOR
C1 (atlas)
C2 (axis)
C3
C4
C5
C6
C7 (vertebra prominens)
INFERIOR

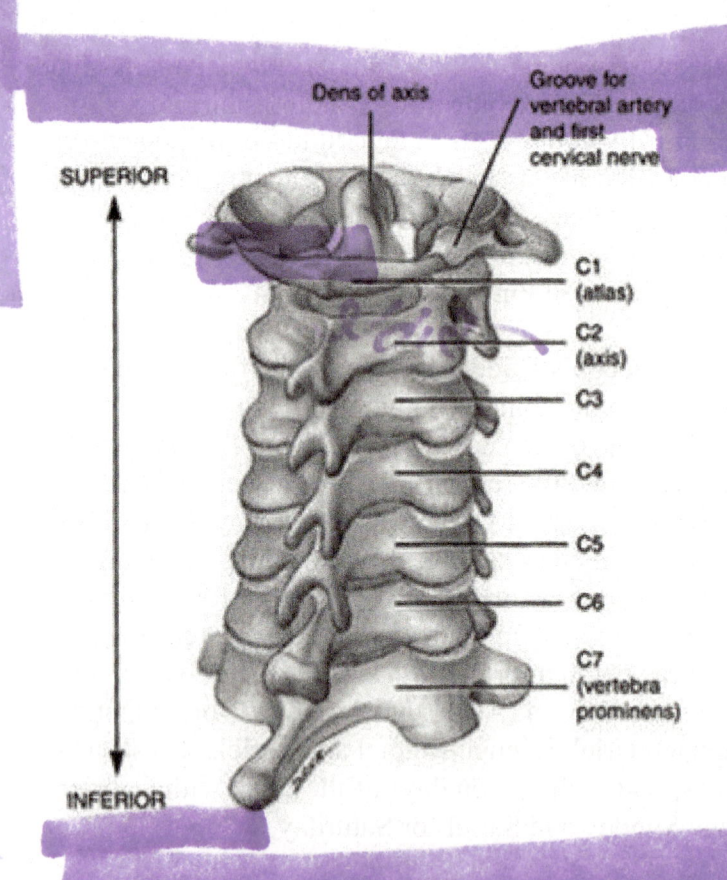

Atlas / Axis

Another idea that is gaining traction is the idea that the spinal column represents the winding staircase of Solomon's temple. [8] The door for the middle chamber was in the right side of the house: and they went up with winding stairs into the middle chamber, and out of the

120

middle into the third. (1st Kings 6.8). This seems plausible however, the author would like to include an additional plausibility that this represents the DNA sequence made up of 23 chromosomes which looks like a ribbon or as the bible says a winding staircase.
[15] For he cast two pillars of brass, of eighteen cubits high apiece: and a line of twelve cubits did compass either of them about. [16] And he made two chapiters of molten brass, to set upon the tops of the pillars: the height of the one chapiter was five cubits, and the height of the other chapiter was five cubits: (1st Kings 7.15-16). Eighteen cubits plus five additional cubits is 23 cubits.

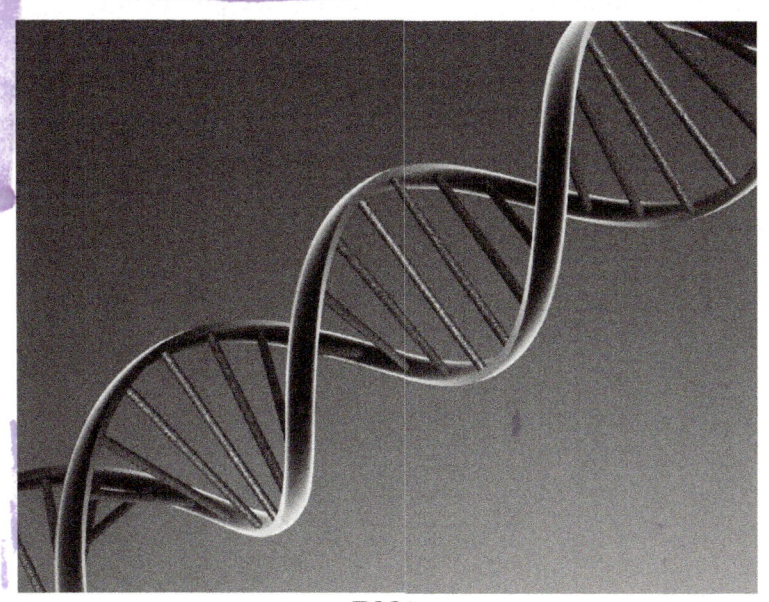

DNA

GOD, THE BRAIN, THE BIBLE AND YOUR BODY

DNA or deoxyribonucleic acid is comprised of five elements: hydrogen, oxygen, nitrogen, carbon and phosphorus. These five elements are directly related to the classical elements of earth, water, air, fire and ether. Hydrogen (H1) is water, oxygen (O8) is air, nitrogen (N7) is fire, carbon (C6) is earth and phosphorus (P15) is ether. Metaphysically they can also be viewed as the star constellation hydra (the snake), oxygen the bull (ox) or Taurus, nitrogen or Aries the ram the cardinal fire sign, carbon for goat or Capricorn, and ether the fifth element or the Elohim principle as phosphorus has the name of the Egyptian sun God Horus. Comparative religious studies has shown us Jesus is equivalent to Horus as both were said to be born on December 25. The 52nd week of the year starts on December 25th and in In Hebrew, the numerical value of the word Elohim is 52 by using the gematria in אלהים: 24+10+5+12+1=52

Manifesting Advice:

GOD, THE BRAIN, THE BIBLE AND YOUR BODY

Yearly Life Cycles

According to the Wisdom of the Mystic Masters by Joseph Weed, we have seven yearly life cycles. The first cycle starts on your birthday, and each of the seven cycles lasts 52 days. (7x52=364). Each cycle corresponds to one day of the week. Beginning with the first cycle called the Sun cycle for the Sun which last 52 days, the second 52 days is the moon cycle, third 52 days is the mar cycle, fourth 52 days or the mercury cycle, fifth cycle is the Jupiter cycle, the sixth cycle is the Venus cycle and last is the Saturn cycle. Once you calculate the 52 days in your life cycle once, you don't have to do it every year because the dates stay the same except in leap years. Weed describes the Moon or first cycle in this fashion

First Cycle

This is the period of opportunity. It is the best time to advance your interests with others who may have the power and influence to help you. This is the time to ask for favors, to seek employment or loans or business concessions, to form partnerships or to make investments. This is also a good time to advance yourself among the people of your city, state or country, to build up your credit standing or your reputation. This is the best time for you to push yourself forward with determination so far as your name, your integrity and your honor are concerned.

Second Cycle

The second period is distinctly different. It is the best time to plan short journeys or trips of immediate importance. It is also an excellent time for moving about, if that should prove necessary. In other words this is a period propitious for changes that can be started and finished within the period itself. In a business way it is a good period for movable things such as freight, cargoes, automobiles, trains, public conveyances, or even public lectures or performances which may move from place to place. It also presents excellent opportunities for those who deal with liquids, milk, water, chemicals, gasoline, oil and other products of this character. Dealing with people who are in business associated with the foregoing will be more successful at this time than at any other. This is also a very good period for businesses which cater to transients such as hotels, restaurants, car rentals and similar services. However, one should not plan a change of business or start a new career or make any permanent change during this period, and contracts and other arrangements that are intended to last a long time should not be entered into. It is an unfavorable period to borrow or lend money and it is not good for starting the construction of a building or entering upon a project that requires a substantial investment. Certainly it is a most unfavorable period to speculate in the stock market or to gamble in any form.

Third Cycle

This period requires that you exercise discrimination and good judgment. It usually brings a great inflow of energy which makes you want to do great and important things.

GOD, THE BRAIN, THE BIBLE AND YOUR BODY

If directed carefully this can be the best time in the year to improve your health or build up your business or do anything that requires the expenditure of energy. However, good judgment is needed. You will be tempted to undertake projects which have no possibility of success or which may take so long to develop that you will have to abandon them before completion. But this is a great time to tackle and overcome obstacles that have blocked progress in the past, to make a strong second effort to solve problems earlier abandoned because of lack of energy. It is a great time for dealing with things that require great energy such as iron and steel, electrical machinery, cutlery, sharp instruments and fire. It is also a particularly good period to oppose competitors or deal with enemies who have heretofore been obstacles in your path. It is an unfavorable period for men or women to try to deal with women but on the other hand it is an excellent period for women to appeal to men when desiring favors or preferment or aid in business or social matters. Arguments and strife should be avoided because the outcome is very apt to be bad, but if you have something to sell which can be put across in one forceful interview, this is the best period.

Fourth Cycle

In this period the mental and spiritual nature is stimulated. It is thus an excellent period for writing books, producing plays, making plans, for all the matters requiring imagination and quick thinking and the ability to express your thoughts lucidly. Your mind will be filled with new ideas which will come very rapidly, so it is important that you grasp them quickly and put them into practice before they are forgotten or pushed aside by the new thoughts which will crowd upon their heels. It is therefore a good period to act on impulse or hunches. You will be optimistic in this period but somewhat nervous and restless, which is to be expected with your imagination highly charged. It is a good period to deal with literary people, writers, journalists, book or magazine publishers, but be careful to scrutinize all legal and other documents most carefully because deception is possible and it is a period when falsehood is as eloquently and easily expressed as the truth. Most great losses through robbery or deception or misunderstood legal situations occur in this period and you should take precautions to protect yourself. However, it is a good time for study and for gaining information and knowledge, but it is not a propitious period to enter marriage, to hire help or to buy homes, businesses or land.

Fifth Cycle

This is the period in which it is possible for you to achieve your greatest success in your personal affairs. This is the time in your yearly cycle when your interests will expand and your prosperity increase. Your mind likewise will become a more effective instrument, sharper and clearer, you will become more open in your relations with others, move with more confidence and display sociability, benevolence and sympathy. This is the best period for dealing with the law, with lawyers and judges, the courts, government officials, men of prominence in the profession and people of wealth. It is also a good period to begin new ventures that may take some time to grow, to plan large business negotiations or to undertake long journeys. It is particularly good for collecting money due or for speculations in stock or real estate, but be sure to avoid every negotiation that is not completely legitimate. Also avoid any dealings in cattle or meat products or with marine affairs.

Sixth Cycle

This is the best time in your yearly cycle for rest, relaxation and amusement. This does not mean that business will not prosper. On the contrary, all good and legitimate business will continue with almost as much success as in the preceding period. However, now is the time to make long or short trips for the purpose of renewing friendships or for cultivating new friends, men among women and women among men, and to renew and improve friendships and relations that already exist. It is a particularly fortunate time for business matters that touch upon art, music, literature, sculpture, perfumes, flowers and personal adornments. It is a good period for a man to seek preferment or favors or business agreement or cooperation from a woman, just as the third period is better for women to obtain such favors from men. It is the best period to buy stocks or bonds for investment and to employ others.

Seventh Cycle

GOD, THE BRAIN, THE BIBLE AND YOUR BODY

This is the most critical period of your yearly cycle. During these fifty-two days the elements in your life that are no longer needed for your development gradually fall away in order to make way for those which are new and better. Often this will cause distress and a sense of loss and may tempt you to foolish actions and decisions. Remember it is a period of seeming devolution which always precedes a period of evolution and new opportunity. Take advantage of the momentum in this period to rid yourself of the old and unwanted, but be sure to exercise good judgment. If there is something that has been hanging fire and is about to end, let it do so, but do not deliberately break ties or destroy relationships that have vitality and are still valuable. For the reasons mentioned, your mind is likely to become despondent and you will be easily discouraged. Remember you are being influenced by the quality of the period you are in and do not permit the pessimism you feel to warp your judgment or inhibit your decisions. The qualities of this period exert very subtle influences and it is necessary that you be much more alert than normal in appraising your feelings and your reactions to external influences. In the Fourth Period it is advisable to seize immediately upon your ideas or hunches and make quick decisions. Now the reverse is true. Impulsiveness will bring disaster. Be careful in all necessary judgments and postpone to the next period every decision possible. However, this is a good period for dealing with older people and those who by their nature or position must consider each action most carefully. It is also an excellent time for inventing things or dealing in inventions or for applying for patents or copyrights. Now you will have success in dealing in real estate, mines, minerals and all things deeply seated in the earth or in hidden places. On the other hand, it is definitely the least favorable time of your year to start anything new or launch a new business or to make new expenditures in an old one. Wisdom of the Mystic Masters, Weed, Joseph, Pages 98-102, Parker Publishing, New York, NY

GOD, THE BRAIN, THE BIBLE AND YOUR BODY

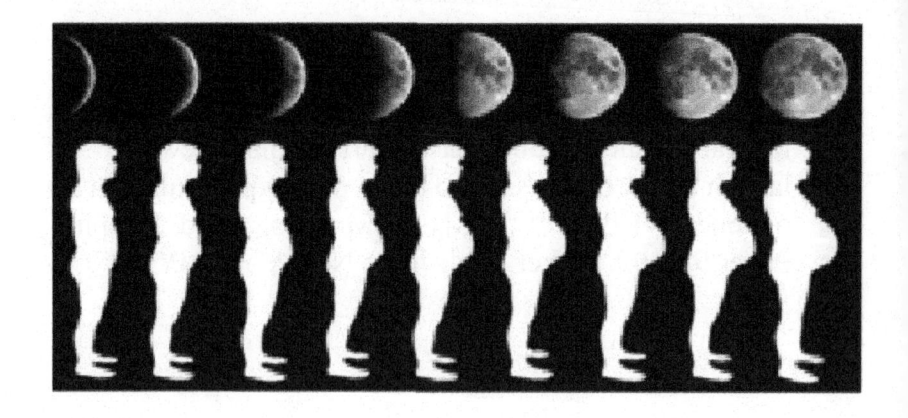

Pregnancy Moon Cycles

GOD, THE BRAIN, THE BIBLE AND YOUR BODY

Another tool the author offers as a method to success is utilization of the moon phases. The ancients used the phases of the moon to coincide with the trimesters of pregnancy as seen in the image. They also knew the different phases of the moon brought certain energies. For example a waning moon was viewed as not so good energy whereas a waxing moon brings great energy. Not to worry you will learn to distinguish a waxing from a waning moon as well as the limitations associated with these different phases. Some easy or early examples would be during a waxing moon it is viewed as a growth phase. Therefore if you want things to grow you would be stimulated during a waxing moon. Waxing moons stimulate the growth of plants which bear fruit above the earth. Another example would be with hair, you should cut your hair in a waxing phase to accelerate growth. Conversely, cutting your hair during a waning period will not stimulate growth it will stifle growth. These things were known by our grand-parents and their parents as they used the Almanac. However, for whatever reason it was not passed down their descendants. They knew by watching the phases of the moon as well as where the moon was in the sky whether to have surgery, when to have sexual relations and other life affecting events such as conception. Women who have problems conceiving a child should try to conceive when the moon is in the place it was at their birth for a higher success rate. Our ancestor passed this information orally we have to now rely on information from others to gain knowledge of this and other ancient practices. According to the article http://www.lunarium.co.uk/articles/phases-of-the-moon.jsp The Phases of the Moon: Their Essence and Astrological Meaning

The New Moon

The Moon is turned to the Earth with its unilluminated side, and so it is invisible to us. Astrologically, we can say that the energy of the Moon is at its lowest point.

This is the starting point of the lunar cycle, and it is believed that new things should be started soon after the New Moon â€" as soon as the thin crescent becomes visible in the sky. If you'll manage to start an activity at this time, it will be supported by the increasing energy of the Moon; you will be as if surfing the lunar cycle.

The day of the New Moon itself is a quiet time, a pause, a time of rest in nature. As it is good to finish off the old stuff before starting something new, the last few days before the New Moon are good for getting rid of everything you do not want to have any more in your life, like bad habits. It is also a good time for fasting as the activity of digestion is at a lower point of its cycle.

In fact, all the automatic functions of the body are at the lowest point in their cycles at New Moon, and this can be a critical time for those who suffer from abnormal blood pressure, who have digestive problems or disturbances of sleep. It would be a good idea to avoid overeating on the day of the New Moon or close to it.

Also, the recuperative powers of the body aren't as active as they can be around the New Moon, and this should be taken into account when planning a surgery.

Similarly, the New Moon can mark a low point in the emotional life, so people who are prone to depression should be careful about the surrounding emotional atmosphere on these days.

The Full Moon

This is the peak of the lunar cycle as the illuminated half of the Moon is fully visible to the creatures of the Earth.

This is again the high point in terms of energy, but the energy of the Full Moon is very different from that of the First Quarter. The energy of the First quarter is like the energy of water running fervently through the pipes in order to get to some reservoir. On the other hand, the energy of the Full Moon is the energy of that reservoir, brimming full or overfilled. It is not that dynamic; there is a feeling of saturation with energy, of having too much of it.

The subconscious is at the highest point in its activity during the Full Moon, and so this is a great time for artists, composers, and other creative people. They are full of images and ideas, and they are usually very busy at this time.

On the other hand, people with an unstable psyche can experience a breakdown during the Full Moon, and there is a substantial body of research showing that the so-called *Full Moon Madness* is the reality of life.

From time immemorial surgeons were advised to avoid operations at the time of a Full Moon, or close to it, as the probability of bleeding and infection is higher than normal at such times.

Pat Thomas also wrote that in some parts of Scandinavia surgeons refuse to carry out operations during the Full Moon believing that blood pressure rises and hormone balance changes making operating more difficult and bleeding harder to stem

The Waxing Moon

When the Moon is increasing in light (waxing), everything in Nature is in the stage of expansion and growth. Therefore, this is a good time for a beginning and an active development of a business.

Cutting hair is advised when the Moon is waxing if you want the hair to grow stronger. However, I heard an opinion that if the hair is cut close to the Full Moon, it will grow faster but at the same time it will become thinner.

In lunar gardening, it is the time for planting anything that produces the desired result (leaves, fruits, or flowers) above the earth.

The Waning Moon

The time when the Moon is decreasing in light (waning) is appropriate for completing things, and for introducing structure and organization into a business.

Cutting hair should be done at this time if you want the hair to grow slower (for example, an epilation).

In lunar gardening, it is advised to plant during the waning Moon those vegetables that give the desired result under the earth (like carrots, potatoes, or horseradish). The last few days before the New Moon are good for pruning and weeding, and otherwise getting rid of everything old or unneeded.

In general terms, a person born during a certain phase of the Moon typically carries the energy of this phase. For example, those who were born close to the Full Moon possess a high degree of intensity and creativity; they are trying to express themselves in one or another way. They can also have physical or psychological problems associated with the Full Moon, such as high blood pressure or disturbed sleep, or inability to relax. Since the luminaries are associated in astrology with the eyes and vision, those born close to the Full Moon can often have a problem with their eyes. Also, the luminaries are associated with parents (the Sun is the father, the Moon is the mother), and since they are in opposition at the Full Moon, there is typically some discord between the parents of the person born then.

GOD, THE BRAIN, THE BIBLE AND YOUR BODY

Those born close to the New Moon are more contemplative, less intense, but they might be prone to depression. I noticed that such people can be often met in an incomplete family — for example, if the mother is a single mother.

First and Last Quarter types are usually very active and dynamic; the former has an emphasis on the personal and family life while the latter is career-driven.

As promised this is how to tell the difference between a waxing and waning moon without having to look it up via electronic means. A waxing moon has the round end towards the right or looks like the top portion of the letter P. A waning moon has the round end towards the left and looks like the round portion of the letter C.

GOD, THE BRAIN, THE BIBLE AND YOUR BODY

Waxing Moon   Waning Moon

Full moons are self-explanatory but new moons are not so easy to identify because during a new moon, the sun and the moon are in the same place in the sky and the luminous portion of the moon is not visible in the sky for two to three days. This is the key to identifying if we are in a new moon phase as the moon will not be visible in the sky. Contrarily a full moon is visible in the sky. Now that you should be able to readily identify the different phases of the moon and you are now know what actions you should take based on the moon phase lets dig a little deeper into how you should use this

GOD, THE BRAIN, THE BIBLE AND YOUR BODY

knowledge. On page 286 of Astrology for Dummies, 2nd edition it states "Make sure the moon isn't in the sign that corresponds to the part of your body being operated on. Thus, if you are going to have surgery on your arm, avoid the moon in Gemini, if you are planning to have knee surgery, make sure the moon is not in Capricorn. And so on." Author's disclaimer: if you need an operation immediately, you need to have the surgery. Please do not put off surgery, however if you can, it is recommended the reader follow the moon when scheduling. Why is this method recommended? The moon has an effect on all water on Earth. As we learned in science, the waxing and waning of the moon affects the bodies of water on earth and gives us high and low tides. The same affect happens in our bodies which has the same percentage of water in our bodies as water on earth. Therefore, the chances of hemorrhaging are greater when the moon is full as well as when the moon in the sign that corresponds to that portion of the body.

So in conclusion, the author hopes the reader receive a better overstanding of the bible, zodiac, chakras as well as helpful tools to enrich one's life and the lives of their loved ones. Meditation, eating right according to the chakras, use of astrology and numerology are but a few of the tools to help set the seeker who has decided to take a long journey on a short path. That short path is the journey inward yet it is a long journey to conquer one's ego. Allowing the ego to grow unchecked keeps the seeker from a life of happiness and bliss and becoming one with the God that is inside.

GOD, THE BRAIN, THE BIBLE AND YOUR BODY

Images

Page 10 - Sarah and Hagar
Page 13 - Oroborous
Page 20 - Virgo
Page 21 - Ptah in the Brain
Page 32 - Side view of the Brain
Page 33 - Top view of the Brain
Page 36 - Kundalini
Page 38 - Eye of Horus/Mid Brain
Page 39 - Great Pyramid
Page 40 - Kings/Queens Chamber
Page 41 - Pine Cone/Cobras
Page 44 - Sistine Chapel
Page 44 - God/Adam/Brain

Page 46 - 33 Vertebrae
Page 47 - Sacrum-Holy Bone
Page 50 - Atlas
Page 51 - Twelve Cranial Nerves
Page 52 - Constellation
Page 54 - Hippocampus/Sea Horse
Page 55 - Ammon's Horn
Page 56 - Amun
Page 58 - Mary Magdalene
Page 61 - Vesica Piscis
Page 63 - Four Beasts
Page 64 - Egyptian Cosmology
Page 66 - Sun Gazing
Page 70 - Power Button
Page 71 - Fertilized egg
Page 73 - Pingala Ida
Page 74 - Khmenu (Ogdoads)
Page 75 - Denderah
Page 76 - Ankh
Page 77 - Triangles
Page 81 - Chakras
Page 86 - Adrenal Glands
Page 87 - Wavelengths
Page 90 - Piano Notes
Page 93 - Baphomet
Page 94 - Skull and Bones
Page 96 - Solomon
Page 99 - Snake Handler

GOD, THE BRAIN, THE BIBLE AND YOUR BODY

Page 101 - Ophiuchus
Page 102 - Ra and Apep
Page 104 - Chakra and Caduceus
Page 104 - Sphenoid bone/Skull
Page 105 - Sphenoid bone
Page 107 - Iatromathematics/Medical Astrology
Page 109 - Nile River
Page 110 - Zjed/Spinal Column
Page 111 - Temple of Man
Page 112 - Dogon Village
Page 113 - Hindu Temple
Page 114 - 3-D Man
Page 116 – Ka'aba
Page 117 - Vatican City / St Peters Basilica
Page 120 – Atlas/Axis
Page 121 – DNA
Page 130 - Pregnancy Moon Cycles
Page 137 - Waxing / Waning Moon

Works Cited

Assmann, Jan. "Of God and Gods", p. 64, University of Wisconsin Press, 2008, ISBN 978-0-299-22554-4

Bailey, Nathan. An universal etymological English dictionary 1773, London, by ISBN 1-00-237787-0. Note: from the 1773 edition on Google books, not earlier editions.

Chevalier, Jean/Gheerbrant Alain. "The Penguin Dictionary of Symbols", p 32, The Penguin Group, 1969, ISBN 978-0-140-51254-0

Gleadow, Rupert, the Origin of the Zodiac, London, Cape 1968, Print

Hall, Manley P. Secret Teachings of All Ages, H.S. Crocker Company, 1928. Print, Page 198.

Kings James Standard Version. Bible Gateway. Web. 1 Feb. 2017.

Mercier, Patricia (2007). The Chakra Bible: the definitive guide to working with chakras. London: Godsfield Press/Octopus Publishing. p. 12. ISBN 978-1-84181-320-2.

Smith, Joe. Shoelaces: A Brief History. New York: Random, 2010. Print.

GOD, THE BRAIN, THE BIBLE AND YOUR BODY

Washington, Marcus. 'Shoelaces and You.' Aglets Daily. Publishing Memes, Inc., 3 May 2013. Web. 12 May 2013.

Weed, Joseph, Wisdom of the Mystic Masters, New York, NY, Parker Publishing, 1971, Pages 98-102

http://www.academia.edu/1618652/Egyptian_fractions_and_the_ancient_science_of_harmonics Web, 17 August 2016

https://www.biblesociety.org.uk/explore-the-bible/articles-about-the-bible/how-can-the-bible-be-interpreted/, Web, 19 December 2016

https://www.blueletterbible.org/search/search.cfm?Criteria=mazzaroth&t=KJV&ss=1#s=s_primary_0_1 Web 5 February 2015.

http://www.dailymail.co.uk/health/article-3992234/Parkinson-s-start-GUT-not-brain-Study-finds-link-disease-gut-microbes.html#ixzz4RiBRc9Rv Web, 2 Jan 2017

http://www.eliyah.com/lexicon.html, Web

http://www.foxnews.com/health/2016/04/26/scientists-witness-flash-light-during-conception-say-discovery-could-aid-ivf.html Web, 10 Oct 2016.

http://www.innerbody.com/image/endo01.html Web, 12 December 2016

http://www.lunarium.co.uk/articles/phases-of-the-moon.jsp Web, 22 Sept 2016

https://www.merriam-webster.com/dictionary/meditate
Web, 11 January 2017.

Printed in Great Britain
by Amazon